Father and Son Influence

Father and Son Influence

* * *

And Many Other Influences

Leroy Jordan Martin III

If you know that you should do better and you do not do better, then you have not come to terms with the power of the Better (God) in you. LJM

ISBN-13: 9781517361327
ISBN-10: 151736132X
Library of Congress Control Number: 2015915489
Createspace Independent Publishing Platform
North Charleston, South Carolina

Dedicated to the memory of Chalena Pugh
A family friend and woman of God, whose passing was difficult to handle, she would usually give me ways to pull from God's word and enjoy a good laugh along the way. I'm appreciative for the times we were able to say "I love you," and the wonderful memories will be cherished.

This book is also dedicated to my first love. My eldest daughter, Imani, through God's power enriched my perspective to become a loving and influential father. Thank you so much for your love throughout the daddy and daughter journey. I thank God for my non-biological son, Decor who enhanced my teaching moments throughout the *father and son* journey.

Table of Contents

Prologue

FATHER AND SON *Influence* (Leroy and J.D.) is only possible because of the true Father, Son and Holy Ghost influence upon my life. I have absolutely no chance of raising J.D. with any impact except for the leading of God's perpetual power, wisdom and sovereignty in my life. I'm also grateful for the many other practical influences that have occurred in my life. The influence of parents, family, friends and strangers is immeasurable. There is an incomparable value in human relationships that empower all of us. In every spiritual and natural influence I will always need the guidance of the Holy Ghost to make it relevant for the next step of the journey. I will forever be grateful to the Lord for teaching me that the father and son influence will maintain its purpose, connection and motivation through the unconditional love of Jesus. My ability to influence my son, J.D., as well as young men encourages me to enhance my prayer life, exemplary living, healthy choices and determination to live in God's truth.

Father and Son Influence developed from some of the great experiences spent with my three- year-old biological son, J.D., during time at home with him daily as a stay-at-home father. I'm also extremely grateful for the tremendous number of influences from so many other people, especially the countless number of young men that I mentor.

This is not a religious book, but it is a relationship, influence and life journey book. Jesus is my guide, hope and Savior. The Master's influence means everything in my life. There is an enormous juxtaposition between religion and relationship. I will not delve into all the details. But the relationship with Jesus is so authentic and pragmatic for the believer. Religion will only give a myopic vision. So *Father and Son Influence* for all men goes to another plateau with a continuous dependence on the Lord's will for our family life. Brothers, we are the spiritual leaders of our home. My daily attempt at a positive, godly and loving lifestyle would unceasingly be in jeopardy without an earnest relationship with Jesus.

The ongoing Southside Chicago shootings that occurred (mainly with African-American men), the Michael Brown shooting by a police officer in Ferguson, Missouri, and the eventual death of the Baltimore, Maryland man, Freddie Gray, while in police custody took place during the writing of this book. So the subject of father and son influence became increasingly sensitive, imperative, heightened and heartfelt on a personal level.

The desire to write this book about the father and son influence was not intended to undermine the equivalent responsibilities fathers owe to daughters. My primary goal is to visit the correlation of father and son influence through teaching consistent values from birth to empower our sons to become men of productivity, valor and compassion, as well as loving family leaders. Unfortunately, selfish errors in my earlier years deprived me of being a better father to my eldest daughter, Imani. Only through God's wisdom was I able to understand the leadership required for a committed family man. This type of influence is possible with determined, courageous and loving fathers willing to trust God to overcome various obstacles in their life's journey. In addition, there are many influences that have enhanced the father and son influence, such as my mother (Chris aka lady love), non-biological father, Chester, sisters Sabrina and Erica, personal mentors, ministers and many other influential relationships. *Father and Son Influence* will address the multitude of influences empowering me to remain dedicated for the long duration concerning the father and son/daughter rapport. Ultimately, I remain steadfast in my belief in a man's ability to become a husband who loves his wife and children based on God's intention for the family.

CHAPTER 1

* * *

Serious Work

Grow Together

I REMEMBER REASONABLY well when my wife gave me the big news. We were going to be expecting our second child together. Although we were not totally surprised, there was some trepidation about adding to the family. What was running through my mind? All kind of things including my feeling that it is going to be tough having another child. We were going to start a brand new chapter in our lives, and we had no idea of the impending challenges. It was time to expand in number and make some serious adjustments in order to grow into a new family.

The time arrived to have an ultrasound and find out the sex of the baby. We wanted to be surprised several years ago about the sex of our first child (daughter), but I did not have the patience to wait this time, especially because I was hoping for a son. I'm not sure if my wife observed my eagerness to look beyond her stomach toward the monitor as the nurse lathered the special ointment onto her stomach. The nurse's hand continued to move in circular motions until she had the perfect position of the baby. It was time for the truth to be revealed. Is it a boy or a girl? The nurse was extremely quick and confident about her announcement. Did I just hear this woman say it's a boy? The nurse confirmed without any hesitation that we were having a boy. Let the celebration begin. The father and son journey has just begun even though he was still months away from being born.

I was ready to begin my influence and growing together with my new son. But I did not have any particular plans for this new journey except to love my son unconditionally and work at being a great father. However, the Lord was equipping my son and me for so much more in this growing together stage.

For several months, my wife did a great job with the prenatal care appointments and taking care of her health. I was able to make all prenatal appointments with our first child and not as many with our son. Therefore, my wife deserves tremendous credit for all the sacrifices and dedication while maintaining appointments for the health of our children.

So the time came for the birth of our son. In the hospital, I felt like a veteran because of my experience as a dad. But we all know that the mother is the real hero, and I earnestly applaud all mothers that put their lives on the line to give birth. I enjoyed being by the side of my wife while she was giving birth, and it was an enormous relief to witness such a qualified and competent birthing team at this hospital. The doctors were very encouraging as my wife pushed through her labor, and all I could do was smile in anticipation of our son. Wow! He finally arrived and there was no greater feeling than being with my wife and new son. When J.D. was born, all the worry, trepidation and fear appeared to dissipate in that moment. Nevertheless, the serious work was now about to begin all over again. I was facing a new work for the first time with a biological son instead of a daughter.

So my wife and I were about to embark upon a new life of influence, sacrifice, love, courage and trust that superseded the previous experience with our daughter, Azaria. Once J.D. was born, it was almost an automatic thought for me to become a stay-at-home father. Although we started a business about six years ago, my wife and I had never seriously discussed the possibility of me remaining at home to take care of our son. How were we going to work this out? In addition, I was in for a surprise, which required me to grow and bond with J.D. in unimaginable ways. The father and son influence became a real-life occurrence. There were undoubtedly some obstacles and precarious situations along the way. Learning ways to handle the uncertainties of life requires ongoing serious work.

During this challenging work as a father, I had to resolve some reluctant propensities. Some of the reasons for my reticence included resources, family time, business goals, procrastination issues and potential missed achievements. Another dangerous tendency in my life has been thinking things are going to be worse than they really turn out. Typically, I experience these temporary invasive emotions before my faith galvanizes and empowers me to override any negative thoughts. In life, we create these false and combative thoughts that are often counterproductive to God's plan. I had to move beyond those harmful thoughts to become a renewed father. We all must encounter uncomfortable times and hardships in this life voyage. Therefore, I was preparing to work through some moderate impediments regarding this new venture with my son.

I had no worries about the responsibilities regarding all the important tasks that needed to be handled when raising a newborn. However, I struggled due to my attempts at becoming a perfect daddy to my new son. Usually when I attempt to do all things perfectly, it backfires on me at some point. There are times when being overly meticulous has been unproductive and unnecessary in my life. I was about to discover ways to become more efficient and effective as an experienced dad while reducing some of the self-pressure. The most powerful experiences as a father were ahead of me, and the time seemed to move quickly. The initial baby stages with J.D. felt like second nature, but now I was encountering the toddler stage.

Feel the Indescribable

It is virtually impossible to adequately describe the feeling of being at home with J.D. daily. One way to express my feelings is the spiritual connection with him. There is nothing like praying with my now three-year-old son and worshipping God while he is at my side. The many activities we engage in, such as riding bicycles, playing baseball and football, racing cars and reading only deepen the chemistry between us. There is no limit to the activities, because it all keeps me youthful and energetic. I enjoy staying busy with him for my own healthy habits. No amount of money, cars, houses, material items or any tangible gift could ever compare to my connection with J.D. Others can have all of the stuff. All of those things are immaterial to me. The love for my children surpasses those temporary gratifications and pleasures. I have an extraordinary gratitude for the father and son influence. The way I feel internally is indescribable.

If I were to attempt expressing my relationship with J.D. from a natural standpoint, I would describe it as an experience of never-ending access with my favorite activity and best friend wrapped together. I actually experience our bond increase and intensify the more time that I spend with him. Shaking J.D.'s hand, saying "I love you," playing games, wrestling and racing one another in the street are all the additional pleasures that enhance the father and son influence. God blessed me with a biological son, and it gave me a new perspective toward fatherhood. Make no mistake about it. All of my children have given me incredible joy, and I'm appreciative for learning so much of the important fatherly duties from them during each stage. But now, how do I evaluate my life as a father?

Self-depiction as a Father

I see myself as a father who enjoys his children immensely. As a father, there are times when I'm too serious for my own good. As a result, there are various adjustments necessary in the fatherly journey. This is an imperative step to me, because I recognize my serious-nature side as a detriment in parenting if I neglect to balance things out with laughter. So I find many times when making changes they create successful results, and other times I have to reevaluate my fatherly actions. Being candid with my children continues to assist me with learning new insight and building on our trusting relationship. I use creative measures to influence within the family.

My children love to play all types of games with me, and I rarely decline the opportunity to spend fun time with them at home. We do everything from dancing, giving rides on my neck, playing basketball and chess, reading, singing, building tents, playing hide and seek and Uno, cooking and other miscellaneous enjoyable activities. In addition, my wife and children highly enjoy their fun time together. At times, my wife and I are unable to be involved in many activities concurrently because of our conflicting schedules. But it feels fantastic when we do take advantage of those entertaining family moments together. Family influence is critical, and I appreciate the positive compliments from strangers when they recognize the effort we have made to inspire our children. People have gone out of their way to mention nice things to me and my wife about our children and family dynamics. By the way, we recognize that we have not arrived completely. Family life demands ongoing learning, determination, struggles, tenacity and hope.

As a father, I aspire to actually practice the things I teach in my home—not always an easy task. There are certainly days when my children experience conflict, and I encourage them to work it out. However, our children benefit from the consistent teaching and exemplary parenting at home. If they conduct themselves in a certain way at home, it will transition outside of the home. So if parents are disrespectful, dishonest, use profanity or reflect other inappropriate behaviors, then it becomes instilled in their children. The parents' positive measure of discipline will not affect their children if they are being set up to fail. Correction is necessary, but we parents need to be sure to take a glance at our personal deficiencies in parenting. I have consistently observed better results with modeling the behavior that I am trying to accomplish with my children. We benefit from identifying shortcomings and taking action with God's wisdom. Do not oversimplify the following point! Influence starts with you.

I'm a very protective father, and many men can relate to being protective over the family. However, my protection extends past the desire to guard my children from physical dangers. In order to be wholly protective, I'm aware of so many subtle things that could impede the purity of my children. So I attempt to remain aware of things I expose them to and the activities that envelop our lives. It is impossible to escape all troubling circumstances, as well as potentially unwise to shield our children from every obstacle. Therefore, I do not encourage any parent to attempt influence in a perfect fashion. I do not equate influence to being an infallible parent. Do not become dreadful over the past errors. We absolutely should refuse to live in fear, entertain it or exert any of its destructive forces. No thanks! *The Lord is on my side; I will not fear. What can man do to me? (Psalm 118:6)*. God intended us to walk, think and live in peace. Therefore, I continue to view myself as a father that learns through personal errors while enjoying new ways to evolve in family life.

Self-depiction as a Husband

I love being in a committed marriage with God and my wife. When we were married by our pastor, Rev. White in Philadelphia, he ministered to us regarding the threefold (pyramid) relationship between God, husband and wife. My wife and I have dubbed it the 2x factor. We enjoy texting one another with the reminder of 2x at the end of the text. It means we are strictly connected in marriage through our ability to remain married to God. We kept our 2x factor learned from premarital counseling to influence us that marriage is absolutely impossible without God being at the top of the pyramid.

I feel so empowered in my role as a husband and head of the family. Although some people have a tremendously blessed single life, I substantially enjoy being a husband. Being a leader, man of integrity, encourager, provider, trustworthy, valuable and adaptable are some of the qualities that I cherish as a husband. I especially take the role of an entrusted leader as a responsibility given to husbands from God. *For the husband is the head of the wife, even as Christ is the head of the church: and he is the savior of the body. (Ephesians 5:23).* But it requires taking an inventory of the total character of the husband. I view myself as a husband who has wrestled with some flaws, challenges, errors and misperceptions about marriage, especially during the early years. I would be willing to share them, but it is too much to cover, and there are some things only reserved for me and my bride. When you release too much confidential information in a careless manner, it could be detrimental toward your intended purpose. There is a time, place and appointed person for spouses desiring to maintain marriages of sanctity. Be mindful of ramifications that derive from irresponsible actions. I encourage husbands to become effective listeners. Wise counsel can accentuate your attributes, influence and position in family life.

For all soon-to-be grooms, you will potentially receive great advice, counseling and ministry from many wise men. And I would like to add that one of the greatest marriage lessons learned in my life was the ability to walk through unprecedented difficulties with my bride. It takes two! I really do believe it takes two determined spouses with an inclination to work through the marriage journey to accomplish the best results. I encourage you that it is absolutely possible to overcome the measureless difficult issues. Be receptive to being compelled. The Holy Ghost influences! The ability to have longevity, success and prosperity in marriage continues to be a concerted effort from me and my wife to endure until the end. I'm grateful toward the Master for placing specific attributes in me and my wife that help our ongoing marriage pursuits. Some of the attributes, such as loyalty, determination, self-control and peace continue to progressively launch my marriage to higher ground. Just a reminder: in marriage, we continue to learn so much and benefit from making important transformations. Be humble! For me, the ability to grow in husband qualities will one day assist J.D. with some of the practical matters of family life. Being exemplary matters! Our sons are learning lifelong lessons from us.

So my depiction as a husband can be put in these words. "The best is yet to come." Being at this stage of marriage ultimately means that I have barely scratched the surface on who I will become as a husband. What are my aspirations as a husband? I have numerous areas to elevate as a husband, especially pertaining to my goals of spending quality time at an optimal level with my wife. Influence means you will honor and guard the words that spill from your mouth. In marriage, you are not able to devolve your responsibilities onto anyone else. The self-depiction prosperity for any husband will flourish when removing selfish agendas and opening up to God's depiction for the husband. In other words, whatever informs the self-depiction really does matter.

Learn from Unplanned Events

Some of the better experiences in my life were developed from unplanned events. The unplanned great experiences include relationships, business achievements, ministry triumphs and life resilience. You really never know your abilities until attempting to try something in earnest. It makes a difference. For some reason, God never allowed me to be a quitter, even during extremely turbulent life experiences and unplanned scenarios. However, do not misconstrue unplanned with irresponsible. I would never advocate being irresponsible, because that may lead to deeper problematic living and thinking. I never planned on becoming a stay-at-home father with all the duties I normally reserved for my wife. But my aspirations to remain committed as a father enabled me to increase my responsible attitude and mindset.

By the way, I have learned to understand and appreciate the equity involved in raising children when a father does his part. What is a father's part? In my perspective, it begins with being a leader as a husband and simultaneously understanding God's intention for the family. In doing our part as fathers, we should remember it is a process. The process of an invested family man will involve highs and lows such as empowerment and discouragement. In addition, there are various oscillating episodes during the family journey. Although there have been extraordinary days being at home with J.D., there are plenty of formidable encounters to balance things out. But I absolutely would not avoid taking on this responsibility again. I better be careful of what I mention, because I never know what is coming down the line. My wife and I find ways to joke about the pathway to our family destination. In the meantime, I will continue smiling, advancing and enjoying all the duties and responsibilities of a family man.

The influence of a family man will be demanding at times, especially when jumping into unchartered waters. I was accustomed to changing diapers because of my oldest daughter, Imani. But the responsibility of feeding, changing diapers throughout the day, functioning on insufficient sleep and holding constant vigilance requires full-time accountability. I certainly applaud all the great mothers that historically took on this role within the family. In addition, I salute the many brothers committed toward unflagging determination to raise, provide and maintain a model positive lifestyle toward their sons for the long duration. Not only do I admire your faithfulness, but your son will be the recipient of lifetime preparation. Brothers, keep on influencing!

Raise the Self

It feels like I'm raising myself when I look at J.D. and reflect on my childhood. Many people say J.D. resembles my physical looks, especially when I was a child. But there are various reminders with his behavior and personality that cause me to reminisce on my childhood. Our commonalities include our walk, smile, modest ways, sensitivity, competitive ways and determination, to name several. More important, I feel committed to helping him grow as an individual and not attempting to make him just like Daddy or anyone else. Sure, there are many ideas and perspectives he will learn from Daddy and other positive men. But I think developing into who God intended us to become allows us to remain liberated in life. So raising J.D. is like I'm raising myself, because I pour into him as God empowers and fills me with His wisdom. There is no restraint in my confidence that J.D. will understand his God-given purpose with my guidance and influence as a loving father. As you assess the characteristics of your son, seek to understand the adjustments that are critical as a teachable father.

Some of J.D.'s other early characteristics include his compassion, humility and honesty. Conversely, J.D., like most children, exhibit behaviors that require correction, consistency and motivation. Be encouraged, fathers, to maintain your composure when feeling frustrated, because you are not alone. You may feel like pulling out your hair. I do not have to worry about pulling out hair because I'm already bald! But I would like to know if any parent has the remedy to making children share toys and other items consistently with their siblings. I need it urgently, so I can give J.D. a dose. I'm willing to purchase it at a high price. Of course, I'm being facetious about such a remedy. The reality is parenting comes with a price of patience, sacrifice, discipline and working on personal flaws. I encourage you to consider your shortcomings and progressively take action. Also, let's make sure the attributes of our sons are being assessed, monitored and enhanced along the way. So let me share in greater detail these early characteristics about J.D.

Show Compassion

I observe J.D. demonstrating compassion on a regular basis. Where does his aptitude for compassion start? Is it something innate or learned in his earliest years? Maybe it is a combination, but I trust some of his compassionate side comes from imitating his big sister, Azaria. Being sort of close in age, he attempts to replicate some of her behaviors. I endorse compassion, because it allows us to show mercy when we could do otherwise. It is worthwhile working on ways to instill a positive influential character in our children and watch them utilize it daily. Azaria does well as a responsible big sister and frequently leads by example, which makes parenting slightly easier. J.D. and I both owe Azaria a humongous hug, and she often gets one from Daddy and little brother.

Smile

One of J.D.'s greatest qualities is his loving smile. My son gives this wide and coy type of smile. He does it when behaving in a sneaky, mischievous or affable manner. I'm sure many fathers notice the same attribute in their sons. His smile is symbolic of his expression to let others know something exciting is happening and you do not want to miss it. Smiles can be infectious. I hope you continue smiling, Son, because someone needs to see a friendly face.

Embrace Competitiveness

Conversely, competition seems to run through his blood. I'm so competitive with games, challenges or anything that I desire to win. So I'm not surprised J.D. is similar with trying to constantly win and detest losing at anything. One of the important jobs for me is to teach him to work through adversity. Our ability to learn subsequent to defeat can put us in a position to attain future success. As a result, I find myself explaining and teaching J.D. ways to learn even when losing as a competitor. The proper mindset is vital for a person's ongoing competitive spirit and winning attitude. If you are always discouraged after losing and you accept that mentality, then it could prevent ongoing growth and moving beyond your disappointment. Why limit your growth and development? The ability to teach J.D. the significance of character development will put him in a position to build on an important life foundation.

It also means we need to regard the welfare and opportunities for others. In my experience, it is not easy compelling people to follow leadership.

It really takes wisdom combined with other qualities. I urge all fathers to never abandon your heart to overcome with all things concerning your sons. Compete with fervor, fire and an unquenchable determination.

Practice Honesty

How do you teach a child to behave in an honest manner? It is not extremely complicated unless you constantly deviate from honesty. If we demonstrate values in a pragmatic fashion, then it comes across in a palpable manner. Just live it. Children tend to catch on quickly. J.D. typically does well with responding in an honest fashion. I do not take this for granted or think his honest ways are coincidental. In fact, I attempt to be creative with encouraging honest responses and behavior from my three-year-old son on a consistent basis.

It may mean that J.D. will be rewarded for his honesty, but I frequently strive reinforcing his truthful responses. Consistency matters! So there are times when J.D. will express to me some of his improper actions without any prompting from Dad. He usually gives me a big smile when he is telling on himself. Then he will proceed with conveying his misdeed of the day. There are times when I turn my face, so he does not see me laugh at some of his honest answers. Now, if I could just get him to stop picking on his big sister all the time!

Many fathers are in a position to be informative, empowering and effective with sons regarding truthful actions. Yes, it requires ongoing teaching and making adjustments as merited. When we are able to guide our sons with the right instruction and practice exemplary living as fathers, then it really works. You too will be held to trustworthy standards as his father. Your integrity and honesty should be the preeminent example for the best results and life lessons with your son. In other words, your son primarily imitates your living. Pay attention, and you will notice his demonstration of your behaviors down to the minor details. In addition, there are too many times when coaches, teachers, mentors and pastors have become the main guide for our sons. In my opinion, they are the ancillary leaders for our sons. These men are certainly essential elements when raising our sons from a communal perspective. Are we aware of our fatherly effect on the future of our sons? Take time to reflect on that question. In fact, I mentioned that question, because I did not realize the depth of my early years of irresponsible choices. Influence from men matters. However, the influence of husbands seeking to understand God's plan for the family delivers powerful results.

As a young boy, I grew up thinking it was no problem to tell certain lies. Some people call them "white" or "small" lies. Those are dishonest ways that are seemingly not harmful to others. Let me set the record straight. There is no such thing as a small or white lie. It is similar to saying Santa Claus is a real person coming down chimneys and dispensing gifts to all children. Sorry kids! It is all made up. Being dishonest is a heavy weight to carry, especially when a person does not realize the internal damage being done. I view lying as the top of my list of character flaws. Do you realize getting away with lies is more detrimental than getting caught in lies? Why? One reason is the ongoing propensity to continue lying. Another reason is putting insidious thoughts in your heart and accepting them. Those two reasons should suffice, and I could certainly create a much longer list.

Guess what? It takes practice overcoming any flaw. In addition, I say to myself that I'm a work in progress and productivity. The day we become complacent with success in any area could be a decoy for future pain and disaster. So I'm uncompromising in my quest to confront dishonesty and beguiling situations that appear not to be injurious or damaging. Subtle distractions are often underestimated and tend to manifest in other areas. I also trust in the power of dealing with the root of the issue. When dealing with the root problems, it is a process that requires time along with diligence. All of this matters, because your influence is entangled in your character. How do you combat deception and dishonesty?

Well, we always have the option of telling the truth. Of course, most of us understand that is the obvious solution. But honesty comes with a price to pay. Be careful not to judge anyone else concerning this topic, because I'm also speaking to those who do not acknowledge their dishonest ways. So I'm implying we need to primarily learn ways to examine ourselves. Whenever we successfully self-examine, we discover things about ourselves that should motivate us to make changes. Being honest is such an important part of influencing our sons to live in integrity.

Over the years, many young men expressed to me the hypocrisy, deception and dishonest actions of parents. If these young people are not able to trust their parents, then it leaves them in an insecure position. I really want you to consider whether your son can trust you and the things you speak to regarding his life. It is disturbing when young men would trust a stranger before trusting a parent. Eventually young people will seek someone to trust, and it may potentially be the wrong person. If this is a current hindrance between you and your son, then being honest and taking action will put you in a position to overcome this unwholesome condition.

Typically, I do not use a specific formula for resolving deficiencies, but I entreat you to really work on becoming trustworthy. It is liberating not being inundated with covering up lies. Your word is all you have at times, and it could dictate whether your children will support you. Furthermore, our reputation as fathers is pivotal when attempting to compel at the highest level. Many people understand that developing a good reputation can take years, but one situation can bring it tumbling down. However, do not quit; rather, trust the Lord to restore you. I will never be able to overemphasize the paramount need of a husband flourishing in family life. Brothers, you are still able to influence, but do not neglect repenting before the Lord. Your son benefits from the values practiced by Dad.

Do you see similarities between you and your son? My son runs like me when he is playing sports. It is so funny to see, because he runs in a wild, fast and determined manner. I still recall my older sister, Sabrina imitating the way I used to run as a little boy. I knew how to put some serious wear on a pair of sneakers. I have no doubt that J.D. will follow in my footsteps. In addition, he is quiet and shy until he warms up to you. But his normal tendencies and personality come to life once he feels confident that he can trust you.

I take J.D. to the library every Thursday for a reading and activities session with children ages three to five years old. One of the librarians reads several books and does fun activities for the children weekly. J.D. usually takes a few minutes to settle in before he participates. The activities include waving their hands and jumping up and down with the other children, along with coloring, reading and fun games. It is the highlight of my Thursday morning. My hope is that he will become increasingly prepared socially for kindergarten in another year and a half. J.D. is doing great up to this point. Although he is quiet natured, J.D. appears to benefit from all the new friends at the library. He even speaks about some of them by name. It is so intriguing to observe children influencing other children. Our weekly time at the library continues to be an important activity to gain social and educational nuggets.

Typical Day with J.D.

A typical day with J.D. involves praying, exercising, watching cartoons, reading, eating food and communicating about anything. Dialoging with a three year old about airplanes, ants, race cars, building blocks, animals and sports can get quite intense. Our sons are willing to discuss anything, as long as we are willing to listen. It really does not matter their age; children need fathers to listen attentively.

I sometimes ask God to assist me with patience to listen effectively. Many conversations with our young sons will be disinteresting to us, but learning to listen to them is valuable to their lives. J.D. constantly wants to know that I'm focused on him. He knows when Daddy is tuning in or tuning out of the conversation. He will swiftly say, "Daddy, did you see that?" If he feels that I missed something important to him, he will express it to me. So a typical day with J.D. means listening first, maintaining focus and responding in a felicitous manner or risk being called out by a three-year-old son. What does your son teach you during the course of the day? Try not to forget that influence works both ways.

Work Out

One of the fascinating parts of my day is being able to work out with my son. It gives us the opportunity to bond in a major way. He and I enjoy spending quality time doing push-ups, pull ups, silly competitive games, racing and performing jumping jacks. He depends on Daddy to be the leader, and he learns so much during our time of exercising together. Consequently, I learn just as much from him during these workout periods. I would have never imagined having the privilege of spending substantial time with my son while helping him to create good habits. The proper foundation for J.D. means a potential advantage over the adversities he will encounter in his life journey. "Keep working hard, Son! The best is ahead of you."

Find Self-identity

I often see young guys make a shot on the basketball court and they give their favorite player credit for a shot they put in the hoop. They will shout, "I'm Lebron," "I'm Kobe," or "I'm Durant!" Of course, I understand they are identifying with the best players on the planet. But they are the ones who made the shot. I would like to hear instead their game mates calling out their names in admiration. As a father, give yourself credit, and make others want to say your name. Why? You deserve it.

So continue working hard, study unremittingly and trust God in all your endeavors. His strength will empower you in a way that far exceeds a career. Never abandon the need to form and develop character traits and skills in every facet of life. Having peace and a fulfilling career is a good combination. By the way, we absolutely benefit from gleaning and learning from other phenomenal leaders. Nevertheless, you are the only one who can be you. Identify with yourself primarily, and you will most likely find contentment in other areas. Seek God for His unflagging guidance in character development.

Undertake Hard Work-work

J.D. and I have a favorite Gatorade commercial that is riveting when it comes on television. There are several athletes throughout the commercial that epitomize hard work paying off. The theme echoes the words hard work-work throughout the commercial. Maybe you can relate to this theme as a dedicated father. My son smiles every time he hears the commercial, and he gets my attention. We immediately drop everything and begin shooting baskets in his junior basketball hoop while singing along with the words, "hard work-work." God made us a great tandem, and this commercial encapsulates some inspiring areas for the father and son influence.

Engage in Self-defining and Characterizing

I frequently reflect about the condition of our youths, especially because of my daily dealings with young people. They are so overwhelmed with image, self-worth, heartache, temptation, instant results, pornography, pain and so much more. What defines or characterizes your child? We should not expect our children to treasure or capture the significance of character on their own. Are you contributing to their value or expeditiously forming their demise in character? If you are concerned with your character deficiencies as a parent, do not give up on modifying your reputation. Let us acknowledge that all parents have something to improve on in life. One helpful idea, especially for fathers, should be our willingness, sincerity and commitment to assist in establishing a positive identity in our children. Indeed, we can become successful in our ability to guide our sons in their character if we continue forming the proper character within us.

This means fathers should exhibit strength and effort in many areas to produce a consistent positive lifestyle especially for our sons. Do not misinterpret my focus on sons. There must be an abundant amount of energy, sweat, prayers, investment and love toward our daughters simultaneously. My focus on sons is drawn from fathers becoming consistent leaders of the home to raise new leaders—boys maturing into responsible men.

If our sons can characterize and define their lives in a positive and godly light, I trust there will be a reduced level of promiscuity, resentment, self-doubt, dishonesty and fear, to identify several harmful conditions. In fact, I think girls and young ladies will define their lives in a renewed fashion because of the treatment from boys and young men. However, this success with our children is contingent on men being leaders of the family, hence, the paramount value and prompting of father and son influence.

Form a Winning Team

If you were forming a team, would you prefer a more athletic person or a mentally focused and committed athlete without as much talent? Wait. Do not give your answer at this point. We will address this question later in the chapter. I found this to be an intriguing question due to my understanding of family as a team.

How can we transform this lack of family continuity, growth and development? The answer is based on your situation. But let us acknowledge one important fact. If our home life is not working, then we need to make some adjustments. Also, leadership really does matter. What type of leader are you as a father? In our striving to become a good leader in our home, it means we will make mistakes. But we should be willing to rectify them along the way and not remain in a position of stagnation. So in my quest of correcting errors, I have found no greater resolution than attempting to practice my faith of the gospel daily. *So also faith, if it does not have works (deeds and actions of obedience to back it up), by itself is destitute of power (inoperable, dead) (James 2:17).* The ability to influence as a family man also positions you to remain attuned to the fresh perspectives from the Lord, even from the most unlikely sources. Listen with purpose.

In my personal experience, I have discovered poor leaders can still have some potential useful influence. How is that possible? It sounds counterintuitive and unintelligent on the surface. It means use all the helpful insight and leave the rest alone. We do not always discover poor leadership or people that lack integrity immediately. I have still found myself on the winning side despite experiencing some unpleasant situations from leaders. As a result, I have used the faith-filled words of influence and allowed myself to forgive the individual. In fact, I can specifically point out beneficial faith practices that have derived from leaders without integrity. When people point me to God's word to assist my life, then it grabs my attention. If they do not value their own words, then it is their loss. In addition, there are times we find out things too late regarding deceptive leaders. Proceed forward and remove yourself from under rogue leadership. I trust that we will not be judgmental when an insidious leader is exposed but earnestly pray for that person. *But I tell you,*

Love your enemies and pray for those who persecute you (Matthew 5:44). In addition, if you feel disconnected from leadership, then it is imperative to evaluate your situation. Also, let us be mindful of assessing our conduct and not always respond in a hasty manner to blame leaders for your inability to concede to authority. I encourage you to remain alert, judicious and patient when selecting leaders in your life.

Personally, several factors put me in a better position to influence, lead and develop chemistry in family life, mentoring and ministry: listening effectively, thinking in a transcendent manner, reviewing past errors and capitulating to God's wisdom and sovereignty over my life. Take the time to create your own list of influencing tools. Once you create it, take time to give serious effort to guarding it, protecting it, valuing it and putting work into truly accomplishing the necessary agenda. Another great help is our ability to gather insight from others to become increasingly informed, instructional and practical within our family. Do not limit yourself. Follow the effective plans, tools, techniques and strategies God has customized for your life. Next, take action.

You can learn from numerous forms of team chemistry in sports and business, as well as other families. Pay attention and consider the benefits offered in unexpected experiences. I gain important insight and understanding especially from young people. Many times it is easy to tune out the ideas young people are expressing to us, in particular if we are trying to impart wisdom to them without listening to their influential gifts. I have learned to talk less at times and become amenable to being influenced. Let me emphasize this point. Stop talking so much and discipline yourself to listen. Influence should not be done in an impudent, harmful or sloppy manner. Yes, it is possible for young people or your child to influence your life. More important, you may learn ways from them to expand your influence over their lives.

I frequently say I do not want my job as a husband, father and mentor to become more difficult than necessary. One solution is to prepare myself continuously while simultaneously teaching those around me ways to become equipped, informed and motivated. Obviously, the latter is the tougher job in most scenarios. So I typically take advantage of opportunities when a young person is receptive to learning, and I attempt to diligently put effort into encouraging his life. In other words, compel other people while they are willing to be compelled.

Now, let's talk about the team member from the first paragraph of this chapter. Would you prefer a more athletic person or a mentally focused and committed person with slightly less talent? I do not think there is a wrong answer, but I want you to consider your requirements and mindset for developing a team. I would choose the committed person with less talent to form my team. My reason is a personal choice. I'm captivated by individuals willing to become better and put effort into improving their lives. So it is easy for me to select the person that demonstrates commitment and a passion to do well. On the contrary, I would not want to have a talented team member who never grows beyond that talent. If you are talented without motivation, then you will potentially remain stuck in the same place in life. There may be some victories along the way for talented people, but they might never envision the greater purpose for their lives. Being satiated without reaching your highest point will potentially taint your mindset and preclude you from striving for heightened aspirations. Give me commitment over the talented individual, and I will have the winning team for the long duration, not because we will win every game but because the mindset to win outperforms the greater talent. Although my inclination for a winning team involves the committed person, talent also has value for any team.

Pay Attention

J.D.'s favorite words to me during playtime are, "Daddy, did you see me?" Watching closely is one of my most important duties regarding the father and son influence. There is a great deal of security, confidence, trust, bonding and growth that takes place while paying attention to the needs of my son. He usually verifies that I'm paying attention to him by turning around to see if my eyes are on him. So I know paying attention is not just for him, but it proves to be an advantage for me while attempting to connect with the mundane actions in the life of J.D. This is beneficial for many reasons, especially when it comes to requesting my son to invest the same attention in me during important teaching moments. He usually demonstrates a willingness to listen attentively and focus on Daddy with some of the more serious issues. Your ability to influence is connected to your magnitude of paying attention to the minor needs of your son. The more trivial, simple and immaterial the game appears to be for us, the more he will require an increased level of attention. I often remind myself that I'm dealing with the mind of a three year old. Unimportant matters really do matter to our sons.

Do not oversimplify this prerequisite to forming an understanding to some of the greater possibilities and intricate pieces to the character of your son. This method of studying your son requires a substantial level of love, patience, honesty, self-control, and authentic interaction. The reward is worth the sacrifice, encouragement and commitment invested in your son.

CHAPTER 2

———— ∗ ∗ ∗ ————

Lasting Standards

Keep Your Head Uplifted

I remember eighth grade graduation at an elementary school in Philadelphia. I was either the first or second boy in the procession because of being so short in school. While walking down the aisle I had my head down. My friend's sister (Tanya) urged me to keep my head up because this was a day of celebration. I recall her saying something like, "Pick your head up. You do not have any reason to be ashamed. This is a day that you need to be proud."

Tanya became an Philadelphia attorney. It is incredible that we recall certain statements that could have a lifelong or lasting impression on our lives. By the way, words can be helpful or harmful for a lifetime. *Death and life are in the power of the tongue: and they that love it shall eat the fruit thereof (Proverbs 18:21).* Even today, I catch myself raising my head if I'm looking down because her words were profoundly meaningful to my life. Walking with your head down could convey a lack of confidence, insecurity or other negative connotations.

In my experience of working with young men, looking down may be indicative of a lack of courage, low self-esteem or an unwillingness to confront life in some cases. I also seriously think that we respond to life contingent on the strength of our mental, physical, emotional and spiritual perspective. So I say, "Keep your heads up, fathers and mothers."

Many things may seem irreparable, dire and frustrating regarding issues confronting our children. But I trust that time, patience and walking in perseverance will deliver a positive outcome. We do have the choice of selecting our perspective concerning all situations. Although life hits us with devastating blows, it behooves us to continue walking with our heads up. Your words continue to imbue me today,(Tanya). You knew ways to encourage young people even during elementary school graduation. Most of us are capable of inspiring others when we remove personal defective outlooks or inhibitions regarding ourselves and other people. Supersede them with substantive thoughts and empowering influence. How do we uplift others if we are giving off the wrong vibe?

The ability to lift others can be a challenging and seemingly insurmountable load to carry. Although I do not believe in the "fake it until you make it" theory, I do think encouraging others will require a high level of discipline. Being disciplined puts us in a position to actively assist others despite encountering some difficulties in our personal lives. We are not able to dismiss every life obstacle just because we uplift, inspire and care for the lives of others. So maintaining the vision and purpose of influencing others means your disciplined life should be used effectively. It is not always easy to move forward when we experience the death of a loved one, sickness, family problems and a host of unexpected negative events. But you and I were born to rise above the most egregious circumstances. The privilege to influence does not terminate due to encountering an unforeseen devastation in our life. Allow the obstacles of life to bring a deeper level of unimpeded influence to others. *A friend loveth at all times, and a brother is born for adversity (Proverbs 17:17)*.

Stay-at-home Father and Mentor to Youth

Some of my greatest responsibilities and tests are the duties of a stay-at-home father attempting to develop a strong bond with my son. In addition, my wife and I have an agency that counsels and mentors youth. It has not always been an easy voyage regarding the tedious task of staying home daily to take care of my son and working with young men in the evenings. It requires a great deal of character, patience, courage, work ethic, trust and love to take on this duty as a committed father and mentor. I give enormous credit to my son for his willingness to assist me with influencing him through his great qualities at such a young age. He makes life easier with his willingness to obey my requests consistently in most situations. I trust the bond, spiritual guidance, prayer life and passion to lead J.D. as an exemplary father enhances his ability to comply with my guidance.

Moreover, the young mentees entrusted to me will always be honored, valued and respected. I owe them so much credit for the personal growth attained in my fatherly pursuits. Young people teach me a great deal when I counsel and mentor them. The father and son influence along with inspiring youths does not work adequately if it is not a reciprocal partnership. Therefore, I remain so attentive to the many young men that continue to go out of their way to encourage me with their powerful words of gratitude. There are times when we set out to give to others, and the inverse actually happens. When you gain good values in your life, then my prayer is for you to motivate the next generation more profoundly.

Embrace Good Values

What are values? One dictionary defines it as "ideals or principles, as of a given society." I spoke on a panel at Regent University regarding Cultural Perceptions: Family Constellations and Societal Implications (February 18, 2014). It was a great opportunity to discuss cultural dynamics especially in the African-American community. There was a statistic that stated more than 70% of African-American children are being born out of wedlock. I did not question the veracity of the statistic, because societal perspectives, goals and values have become intertwined with various agendas and opinions. But I was very disturbed by the number of unwed black parents. Conversely, there are a good number of committed and loving African-American parents. I can think of several African-American friends that influence me because of their diligent fatherly actions and commitment as husbands. For the record, all cultures suffer from this devastation of children being born without married parents or with broken families.

I refer to broken families as those facing divorce, separation and parents living independently from one another and their children. There are many reasons for this epidemic that are not limited to one particular culture. How do we prepare and equip ourselves as husband and wife to endure to the end and take earnestly the vows we made with God? Better yet, what happened to our aspirations to marry, remain monogamous and raise children? Could there be a correlation between current failed marriages and young people being unenthusiastic about future married family life? I'm sure people will respond with various answers to this question depending on one's experience and notion of marriage or single life.

I absolutely learned some valuable insights from my non-biological father that continues to be helpful in my family life. Chester was a great provider, determined leader, fantastic cook, humble, affable and wise. As a result, I have absorbed his wisdom along with attributes from the Lord to unceasingly work toward a solid family life. Quitting is not an option, and there is a considerable amount that I need to learn, even after nine years of marriage. I also give abundant credit to my wife for toughing it out during some early struggles. Wise counsel was beneficial for our ongoing progress and pragmatic approaches to family life. I'm so grateful for early influences, which empowered us as a married couple to ardently work toward transforming our mindsets.

What about young men growing up in a torn family environment? I do not think we should undervalue the type of influence that occurs because of a lack of role models from committed husbands and fathers. In case you missed this vital point mentioned earlier (see the section about fathers being the head of household), husbands are to be leaders, and without his godly influence, the family faces instability and disarray. For every young man who overcame the odds of an unstable household, I applaud your endeavors, commitment and fortitude. Now, I encourage those same men to be the revolution for your sons. My perspective on the revolution describes a man of courage, love, trust, peace and a man after God's own heart.

Of course, we can attribute various problematic circumstances as the reason societal values are changing, diminishing or missing. The lack of values are connected to pornography, poor leadership, violence, lack of role models, substance abuse, hate, lasciviousness, promiscuity, irresponsible parenting, disrespect and so many other issues. Take your pick. The problems are not going to disappear on their own. I choose to confront the lack of values in our families and communities for the sake of our sons, daughters and their peers. Yes, it will be a formidable fight for the family. Now is not the time for cowardly thinking or fickle fathers. Take a stand for the future of our children.

We frequently think of our own children and not the children within the community. Who do you think will have the most influence on your children when you are away from them? Think about it. My contention is that we have abandoned or neglected our propensity for caring about our community. The values that you lack sharing with your neighbor's children perpetuate a value-less community and society. Are you afraid to care and trust in the value of a community? Could it be some other value deficiency in your heart? We can look at many troubled areas in society to see its effect on relationships within families, communities and worldwide. Selfishness and envy have been destructive methods used to rip away our good values and hope for a productive community and society. We have a fight in front of us. It is vital to fight the battle tenaciously, earnestly, judiciously and with courage. What happened to the idea of a "village" raising our children mentality? In order to adequately answer that question, it will require some in-depth dialog, wisdom and an ample amount of time along with work.

Teaching good values is imperative, but being an exemplary parent leaves no doubts in our children's minds. We have all heard the saying, "Actions speak louder than words." Staying at home with J.D. has taught me the substance of those words. It's paramount to live an honest, meaningful and productive life. As men, we should understand the value of keeping our word. If you say something, you need to seriously attempt to accomplish your objective and intended action.

The emphasis is on *action*, because we spend too much time talking about things we never intend on getting done. Poor habits, hypocrisy, deceptive behavior and lack of integrity are some of the contributing factors to our downfall when attempting to empower and influence our sons. The great relief is that young men are forgiving and genuinely love their fathers, as mentioned to me many times as a counselor over the years. Unfortunately, many negative actions have been generationally passed down and have created some of the defective relationships between fathers and sons. Anything broken has the potential to become regenerated, restored and refurbished. Relationships, too, are able to experience this renewal. Keep your chins up, fathers and sons.

Become an Efficient Father

We do not have time to waste concerning the condition of our sons. We can look in every part of the country to observe the lack of preparation, respect, love, trust and peace among our sons. I want to use the city of Chicago as my example of our sons facing disheartened times. In 2014, the African-American community in the South Side of Chicago was suffering because of the ongoing violence. Can fathers make the difference regarding those horrific circumstances? Many of us would answer in the affirmative. We need fathers who are willing to teach love, peace and a multitude of values to our boys in the South Side of Chicago as well as the suburbs of Virginia and everywhere in between. Our sons benefit from appropriate leadership, love and internal investment in the early stages of their lives. It proves to be a game changer in many instances.

As African-American men, we also understand there are some ongoing problems that stem from the many things experienced in our history. Furthermore, all cultures of young men are facing seemingly unprecedented spiritual, emotional and mental darkness. But we seek to make progress and refuse to allow our sons to succumb to worse conditions. I not only believe in our ability to move forward, but our sons are relying on committed family men to assist them in their transformations.

Provide Leadership

My son, J.D., continues to enhance my understanding of the significance of leadership as a father. By definition, leadership is the ability to lead or guide others. That sounds simple enough. However, there is more to it. As fathers, some of our ability to lead is determined by our leadership skills, men who imbue our lives (extremely vital), hope, understanding and the heart to stand on God's word. Certainly, we can use additional pragmatic teachings to lead our sons. Those are five qualities of leadership that have personal meaning to me. All fathers can benefit from a personal list of essential qualities for leading your sons. My personal list for leading and influencing J.D. may differ from another father's, but my leadership is only possible because of my love for Jesus. What is the origin of your leadership? The impact of a loving husband and family man is extremely valuable for our children and the community.

I was raised by my mother and non-biological father. Chris and Chester Wise were together for more than 30 years. He had a tremendous influence on my life and an abundant effect on the way I raise J.D. There are several qualities my non-biological father passed on to me, such as a strong work ethic, patience and courage, as well as endeavoring to always make progress in life. My favorite quality about Chester Wise—and possibly the most effective—was his determination to lead as a family man. He typically taught from a practical manner ways to love, provide, trust, overcome obstacles and give to others unconditionally. He did this without using many words. The truth of the matter is we are constantly learning profound insight without realizing the depth and power until our test arrives. Now J.D. is in training to become a loving, respectful, honest, caring, productive and trustworthy father. The Lord is guiding our father and son footsteps throughout this voyage. All aboard!

Conversely, leadership among fathers, as well as childless men, appears to be fading, defective and depleted on some levels. I do not feel hopeless, because we still have great family men in our midst. I'm enormously grateful for all of the brothers attempting to make a difference within family life. However, the influence has lost some of its sting among father and son. Where do you turn for influence among men? Can you depend on your father, uncle or brother? Who do you choose as a dependable leading man in your life? Are you satisfied with the leadership of men in your community? Ruminate on those questions, and think on other questions relevant to the leadership of men.

There is an urgency to prevent further destructive relationships among men within our families and especially with our sons. We benefit from thinking with a transcendent mindset and alleviating the defective vision and lost perspective of leadership among men. Do not take my word on this issue. Survey your household, community, city, nation and world to make an intelligent deduction on the impact of male leadership upon our sons. The problem regarding leadership of fathers extends much farther than its effect on our sons. What about the impact on daughters, women and the family structure? I firmly trust in leadership and the influence of men as an essential focus for the wholeness of our communities. Why? We are the leaders of our wives and children. When the leadership of the husband is neglected or completely absent, then disarray will ensue.

I do not want to be careless by not highlighting the pervading pain females have endured because of our lack of leadership as men. Yes, I do understand that wives play a significant role in the stability, prosperity and productivity of our families. For now, I'm concentrating on the influence of the husband. The influence of a man matters. I certainly trust that the value of a husband and family man will put our sons in the best position to prosper. Some of my most important teachable points for our sons include these: 1. Love females in a godly manner. 2. Develop friendships without pursuing a physical or sexual relationship. 3. Respect Mom (fathers should be exemplary in this area). The aforementioned principles for our sons are not in any specific order, but they are valuable teaching points from infancy. I emphasize infancy, because fathers should invest quality time from day one to reap the greatest benefits for our sons. We have no time to behave in an inefficient, irresponsible or unintelligent manner. Fathers are instrumental in assisting our sons with achieving necessary goals, values and principles. Men, if not us, then who will adequately do the job? Better yet, let us subscribe to the proper order that God intended for the family. In other words, the husband is critical in leading, influencing and transforming the family dynamics. Pivotal influence for the family is not fully activated when you are developing the foundation on personal strength, pride and self-determination. So let me address the three teachable points enumerated in this section.

Love Females in a Godly Manner

Brothers, have you ever attempted to love a female in a godly manner? It is a powerful experience. Loving females in a godly manner means we honor, love, protect and provide them with the intimacy reserved through Christ. The intimacy is strictly plutonic, and it does not harm or create room for sinful activity. All fathers need to set this atmosphere as a tool for their sons regarding future relationships with females. Why? Our sons need to know women are a treasure given by God and appreciated by men.

Unfortunately, young ladies are too frequently viewed as physical beings exclusively given to pleasure the male's sexual appetite. Our sons need the advantage of thinking about young ladies and women with a renewed frame of mind. I absolutely salute all the young brothers who respect females without abusing them or who are constantly out on the prowl for the next sexual victim. It is not always an easy job, but your hard work and influence have not gone unnoticed. You are respected by many fathers, and I commend you greatly.

Who needs to assist our sons in transforming their thinking toward females? 1. Every father who understands the hate, disrespect and toxic living being conveyed to our sons concerning females. 2. Men who created pain in the life of any woman. 3. Every father who needs to empower, enrich and inform daughters. 4. Every man who never loved or received love from a woman. There is a considerable amount of men in this category. Do you understand the total picture regarding females? If we understand the message in its entirety, men will strive for godly marriages and lust-free male–female relationships. In addition, we will communicate to our young men ways to emulate loving, committed, scrupulous, faithful, and action-oriented behavior. What type of father are you? Trust God for your growth. He is able. *I can do all things through Christ which strengtheneth me (Philippians 4:13).*

I do not want to be negligent in expressing the necessary growth required for all married men, as well as the unmarried brothers. Being married will not automatically reduce the temptations of seduction and satiating the flesh. The perpetual work as exemplary married men is crucial. I trust that we understand the real work of integrity is done when nobody is looking. I really want to emphasize utilizing the spiritual disciplines and other beneficial qualities with which the Lord empowers us during the testing times. I promise you that He always gives us a way out, and we benefit from adhering to His direction for our lives. *There hath no temptation taken you but such as is common to man: but God is faithful, who will not suffer you to be tempted above that ye are able;*

but will with the temptation also make a way to escape, that ye may be able to bear it (1Corinthians 10:13).

It may be a sly look or other subtle maneuvers, but I encourage you to allow God's power to assist you in not entertaining the self-distractions and marriage terminators. We do not always recognize our inclination for destructive influence, even though we still maintain a family life. Take time to reflect, embrace and bathe in God's wisdom to confront moral defects. Remember, we are all human beings, and anyone is subject to falling because of our humanity. Treating our wives in a respectful and loving manner exhibits tremendous guidance for our sons. However, it really demonstrates credibility as a husband when you respect her away from the home front and in secluded environments. Anybody can display a factitious integrity when people are watching you. Do you follow the point? I trust that your positive actions away from the home will mainly ignite the influence of your son. Why? You are genuine and full of integrity. Your son will recognize it, trust you and seek your prudent ways. I deeply appreciate the brothers for doing the right thing, because they love their wives. If any brother has fallen, keep your chin high and completely trust in God's resolution. You can attain great family success, and there are many brothers willing to compel your life.

Develop Friendships without Pursuing a Physical or Sexual Relationship

It is never too late. We can always expect, experience, and encounter God's best for our lives, even during the most unexpected times. My first non-sexual female relationship occurred with my wife. I apologize if that is too much information. I truly believe expressing this will be an influence for other men.

Primarily, my wife and I aspired to concentrate on a friendship during our courting days. We certainly battled some temptations regarding premarital sexual relations like any normal human being. By the way, temptation is not a sin. The willingness to follow through on your immoral actions is how you can become trapped in the darkness of life. Evidently, God was preparing me for this non-sexual journey with my wife. The Lord empowered me for seven years to escape the promiscuous lifestyle prior to marrying my true love,

Devina. I strongly implore anyone attempting celibacy to acquiesce to God's will for your life. His answers to your queries will provide simple, pragmatic solutions. But you are required to make the final choice.

We will usually experience the natural tendency to become physical or sexual before entering marriage. God always provides a counterattack. During my seven years of celibacy, God revealed a simple resolution. Do not empower self-temptation by being alone with women. It sounds simple, but it requires action and application. I became better once I became accustomed to it. We should be reminded to never let our guards down. People frequently make the error of believing they have arrived at the culmination of success because of temporary or ongoing achievements. Be careful of premature celebrations. There is nothing wrong with encouraging yourself previous to success. However, please do not become misguided, uninfluenced or counterproductive toward God's perspective, purpose and plan for your life.

Our sons are depending on us to stay committed for their sake. Your grandchildren will also love you for your ability to endure, teach, transform, foster hope and choose prudently. The generational prosperity, integrity, purity, love and faithfulness will begin with your determination to set the foundation for the unseen generations. Will you make the sacrifice?

Respect Mom

I trust that respecting Mom will come naturally for most sons when they are observing it consistently from their fathers, hence, father and son influence. I will speak from experience in saying my non-biological father, Chester, was such a powerful example regarding respecting my mother. Remember, no individual is perfect. So we should not place undue pressure on our lives. Every husband and wife experiences challenges, and my parents were no exception to the rule. However, Chester consistently gave me a strong example of how to walk away, think and make judicious choices in the midst of difficulties. He demonstrated some good examples of respecting my mother in the home. As a result, I absolutely replicated some good choices in my marriage because of Chester's role modeling as a husband. Conversely, I have spoken to some men who have suffered in making poor choices in marriage because of the behavior witnessed firsthand by their fathers. Influence matters! What influence will you leave as a legacy to your son?

Discover the Influence of a Wife and Mother

Mothers are great contributors and equal assets in influencing and raising our sons. Reflect on the attributes gained from your own mother. I remember as an adolescent one of the long-lasting and profound teachings from my mother pertaining to avoiding salacious relationships. She witnessed an inappropriate situation concerning me, and she admonished me for my poor judgment. She took the time to express that if a female is willing to be rogue toward her boyfriend, then she will produce similar treatment and behavior with you. I was no older than 14 at the time, but my mother's advice still remains vivid in my memory. The wisdom and influence of a mother is priceless.

My mother was conveying not only the important qualities about females but the need to keep relational values in my heart for future reference. Unfortunately, in many cases I chose to learn the hard way. But it is never too late, and eventually I surrendered to God's message through my mother. Despite the seven years of evaluating, I really did seek and discover some similar qualities in my wife. Mothers know the needs of a son, too. My wife and I are going on 10 years of teamwork, chemistry, love and prosperity. Along the way, we did not quit when we encountered setbacks, failures, insecurities and obstacles. In order to reach our influential destination within our family, we will need to outlast the vacillating and capricious journey. My bride was worth every challenge. I'm grateful for the influence of my mother's wisdom and for a virtuous wife.

Without the love, support, understanding and commitment of my lovely wife, I could not be a successful father. My wife is not only my friend, lover, encourager and greatest cheerleader, but she is an equal partner in God's plan for a whole family. The influence of a wife matters. Husbands, let us express our love for ordinary, extraordinary and God-appointed wives through our actions.

As men, it is vital to do the right thing toward our wives. J.D. already watches and responds to my relationship with my wife. He is absorbing my behavior toward my wife at such a young age. Incredible! His capacity to lead as a good husband one day will be firmly contingent on my commitment as a respectful and loving husband. By the way, your son is emulating you, too.

Are we content with our treatment, behavior and expression of love toward our wives? We benefit from thinking in a transcendent manner. More important, we must act in a transcendent manner. Our sons' response to females is frequently connected to Daddy's example and attitude toward women. Make sense? Most definitely, he will be his own person. Nevertheless, one should not devalue nor undermine a father's ability to teach his son through his actions. Try unselfishly not to set your son up to fail due to your conscious or unconscious desire to teach impurity, lust, ego or reprehensible leadership. J.D. would say it takes hard work-work. I agree, and it applies to me, too.

As a man, I must first state some of my shortcomings. The great gift is there is no condemnation because of Christ. You do not have to reduce your life to be a miserable and worthless individual due to former poor choices. I refuse to remain stuck. We should acknowledge, confront and lean on God for the resolution to our various life deficiencies. We are seeking, pursuing and investing in the potential wholesome character of our sons as exemplary fathers. Do not deceive yourself by thinking you have mastered all that this journey has to offer. Maintain stable thinking, character and adherence to God's intention for your heart. What did God help you to identify as a shortcoming in your life? Do not be afraid to confront any problematic leadership choices.

The sooner we address those weak areas, the better our chances of navigating through the course. Earnestly think and reflect on it. We can mitigate, resolve and ultimately become free from the burden of being enveloped by deceitful living. At the minimum, we can learn ways to examine our lives and attempt to move forward. J.D. compelled me to address some painful life events before I could make significant progress as a man and father. God gives us the precise people to encourage us, and I'm grateful for J.D.'s influence in my life. Now, it's time for you to look in the mirror and identify some troubling areas.

I'm not exempt from the list of poor leadership, unpredictable behavior, unintelligent decisions, pain, promiscuity, and outright living a destructive life. Do you think about your life without some of the harm caused by self or others? Did I have to travel down an often difficult and troubled path?

In most cases, it was our choice to journey on the rugged pathway. There are many faults, errors, and distractions many of us have brought on ourselves. I'm no exception, and I do not plan on detailing every specific problem, error and malfeasance of my life journey. It is not necessary, and there is too much to cover. When you are pursuing the purpose of God, you no longer have to feel guilty about former worldly and ungodly pursuits. *There is therefore now no condemnation to them which are in Christ Jesus, who walk not after the flesh, but after the Spirit (Romans 8:1).* Similarly, it is important to share, engage, uplift and motivate other men attempting to become free. Men benefit from the influence of good leading men, especially prior to becoming new fathers, husbands and family men.

Find a Purpose

I think we often miss or neglect our purpose of influencing others due to multiple reasons. One particular reason is being enveloped by selfish agendas. We do not move beyond our shortsighted tendencies at times, because we are too consumed with selfish motives. Our purpose can become very limited, myopic and defective without identifying with the greater purpose that God has for each of us. If your reason or intention for living is not attached with a resolve to flourish personally and for others, then continue seeking your purpose. Do not give up! When we understand our purpose, I trust that we put ourselves in a position to achieve and influence at our apex.

Invest in Sons

What does it mean to invest in our sons? What specific things should we invest in our children? And how long should we invest in our sons? Allow me to work through these important questions as you ponder your answers regarding investing in the life of your son.

Investing in J.D. means I have taken the time to value and put effort into developing his future mental, physical, emotional and spiritual wellbeing. I believe our understanding of who God called us to be as fathers matters in our ability to invest in our sons at a maximum level. So investment in J.D. requires me to bear the responsibility of preparing, listening, learning and relying on God for the best outcome over a long duration. We are mandated as well to be precisely as effective, committed and dedicated to our daughters. What does your investment list look like?

There are a few things that are unavoidable in my investment with J.D. There is no limit, but personal experience plays a role in my investment selections. I will invest in his ability to honor, love and respect women as a godly man. Men, I trust our capacity to witness our sons' godly treatment toward females comes mainly from our direct dealings with our wives. We are now in a position to teach, think reflectively and make essential adjustments to our fatherly investment as merited. I truly have confidence that the following statement is part of the purpose for father and son influence. "The privilege of raising a more informed, faithful and family-oriented generation of men is through men committed to serving their wives and children." What do I believe will ensue from father and son influence? We can begin raising sons that far exceed our understanding and workmanship toward family life. What else? Fathers can experience an increased level of investment with our sons toward the next generation of sons—our grandsons.

The investment from my non-biological father lasted until his death. He was still pouring into my life even when I became a married man. Yes, it was in a different way, but he continued to pass on his wisdom and love into my adulthood. It really had meaning and purpose at the time and especially in my earliest years raising J.D. I will not forget the resounding words of Chester: "You never know what you are going to have to do in life." Chester's last name (Wise) was suitable for him.

How do you influence your own children? It is a difference between what you intend on doing with them and what you actually do with them. When we watch carefully the actions we are doing, it may be surprising to witness some of our shortcomings. There are things we prioritize, which have not consistently wrapped themselves in substance or longevity. Your wants do not necessarily equate influential action.

CHAPTER 3

***

Making Adjustments

Accept Apologies

BUT IF YOU do not forgive others their trespasses [their reckless and willful sins, leaving them go, and giving up resentment], neither will your Father forgive you your trespasses (Matthew 6:15). There are times when sons can influence fathers. If you are receptive enough, you may encounter a strong level of influence from your son. What qualities have you learned regarding your son's personality? Does he remind you of yourself in any cases? I found myself tuning into my son's aptitude to frequently say "it is okay" when confronting a problematic situation in his life. J.D. will usually accept the apologies of others without being reserved and he is willing to move forward. In some circumstances, he swiftly moves on with life despite the wrongdoing that occurred against him. I enjoy that particular quality about him, because many things can keep us in the muddy waters of life. I appreciate the action of a three-year-old boy being equipped and willing to teach his Daddy ways to prevent becoming entrapped with limited thinking. Influence can emanate from a small child or an elderly person. But it is up to you whether you are willing to accept the source of influence. J.D. continues to give me a different perspective, and he assists me in moving from querulous habits. Now, it is time for Daddy to attempt some new habits.

Are we willing to start new habits? This is not always an easy journey as a father. However, in my estimation, it is essential for a productive father and son influence. The opportunity to delve into fresh concepts while raising our sons should not be impeded by our unwillingness to mature in character. Father and son influence is a two-sided relationship. There are deficiencies we will constantly inject into the lives of our sons if we do not identify our poor habits and do something about them. Influence will occur whether we like it or not—negative or positive! What type of influences are you encouraging through your actions? God's word is instrumental in teaching us to concede to renewed fatherly habits. Subsequent to yielding to new habits, we benefit from practicing them on a regular basis. What good is it to have the wisdom and not use it for our father and son influence? J.D. taught me to implement new ways to move forward, because he accepted apologies and continued to make life progress. What does your son compel you to do? Watch your son intensely, and he will teach you. Are you committed to becoming a humble student?

I have failed various times while reproving my son, when I should have listened more and made necessary personal adjustments. Do not waste time beating yourself up for errors. Repent and keep moving. I am especially candid about certain personal errors, because they may position other fathers to become liberated from mental incarceration. The ability to influence will entail some vulnerability. No self-condemnation! No fear! No reticence! When you are genuinely attempting to make progress in an area, then you will release unnecessary life baggage. The importance of becoming a quality listener, student and leader as a father is extremely valuable. During my more studious times as a father, I have learned to become increasingly patient, forgiving, apologetic, trustworthy and action-oriented. The best part about attaining additional fatherly attributes is the contagious impact on J.D.'s life. The popular saying "like father, like son" is very relevant in our influential methods as fathers. Your son will follow in your path; just lead him with all prudence from the Lord.

Practice Patience

I really considered myself a patient individual prior to staying at home with my son. However, J.D. exposed my weakness as an impatient man who needed to learn from his son. There are times when I raised my voice at my son, because I did not take the time to make important personal changes. We are frequently unaware and unclear of our tendency to struggle, because we do not always take the time to work on ourselves. I had to take some rudimentary lessons from J.D. and begin to make gradual changes in my teaching style. Some of the lessons included saying "yes" to my son instead of "yeah." Why? Because children regurgitate what we convey, and then we are surprised when they model us. I had to spend time looking him in the eyes and talking to him as opposed to keeping my back to him without concentrating on our dialog. When we fathers endeavor to gain a measure of success with our sons, then nothing substitutes for taking the initiative and leading by example. Fathers, do not allow ego to get in the way of surrendering to the appropriate behavior toward your son. Your son is not only observing, he will respond according to the way you teach and lead him in life.

Maintain Honesty—It Pays Others

In September 2014 I found a wallet with a substantial amount of money, debit cards and other valuable information. There were also pictures of children in the owner's wallet. Subsequent to searching the wallet to locate the individual, I was able to speak with the owner of the wallet. He expressed a deep gratitude toward me for being honest and returning his wallet. He conveyed to me over the phone, "You do not know how many people you impacted by returning my wallet." His words had such meaning for my life. It encouraged me to make greater personal adjustments. Words could not explain the joy this man experienced, because I gave back what already belonged to him.

God helps us to do the things that are right in His eyes. It does not call for rewards, recognition or boasting about the matter. Our situation may be dire, but giving to others empowers our character, commitment, dependability and integrity. Coincidently, my son and daughter were in the car with me when I found the money and wallet. Teaching the right motives may come when you least expect it. Be prepared to give more without looking to receive. This is what my action showed J.D. and Azaria who was seven years old at the time. Children, I encourage you to continue maintaining your hearts to give to others. Daddy is being influenced, transformed and capable of making paramount adjustments because of your trust in him.

Respond with Kindness when Kindness is Not Returned

At times, your acts will be unrequited by others. Do not become disheartened or direct your conduct according to the response of others. It could potentially create a malfunction, misdirection or misery in the calling on your life. Do not forfeit your ability to support, encourage and influence the lives of others despite the lack of reciprocity. In fact, it feels so much better not looking for something in return. It means you are in a position to act with the proper motives. When it appears that your deeds go unrequited, unnoticed or without purpose, then it is prime time to continue down this journey. Influence finds a way to become motivated by the unseen (Holy Ghost). *But without faith it is impossible to please him: for he that cometh to God must believe that he is, and that he is a rewarder of them that diligently seek him (Hebrews 11:6).*

Beware of Assumptions

Assumptions can be some of the most poisonous influences driving our lives. It is so dangerous to live life consumed by not having factual information prior to speaking or acting. We witness a myriad of ways assumptions destroy relationships and foster unhealthy environments within a family and other vital connections. In particular, children become the recipients of practicing the bad habit of assumptions. It breeds irresponsibility, lazy thinking, gossiping, dishonesty and false accusations, as well as sullies reputations along with the maligning of character. What is your list for defective conclusions without factual information?

Most of us are guilty of assuming things about others. In some cases, it is just a matter of reflecting on your daily dialog and engaging in the social media age. Nonetheless, assumptions can also be a destructive and harmful response to an inner struggle in our lives. Adjustments need to arise if we are going to overcome these moral debacles. I was able to recognize this deficiency in my life and desired to seek God's wisdom on repairing this faulty characteristic. I'm still a work in progress and productivity—no premature arrivals. J.D. is an enormous motivator for me learning ways to address this weakness.

My son is constantly emulating the things he observes from my life. By the way, so is your son. Trust me! My choice to eliminate this poor quality of defective conclusions (assumptions) was partially to enhance my positive influence on J.D. I really did not want to continue making the same mental errors and practice the same poor habits while setting my son up for future failures through assumptions. Some may say change is hard. I concur with that thought. My next response is to check out the alternatives and options.

Frustrations, poor health, rancorous mentality and insecurity are some of the setbacks of not confronting our weaknesses. I readily acknowledge that working on removing assumptions in my life continues to be a great advantage. You can increase personal progress when you practice a goal, quest or pursuit consistently. I encourage you to seek God for the adjustments you should make in your life.

Let me mention an important note at this point. There are critical things in our lives that we will never overcome without completely and earnestly yielding to God's will. Think about it. You may not struggle with making assumptions, but you have some area of weakness. Is it possible to release and attach these deficiencies to our sons? Take the time to ponder and respond to that question. More importantly, the toxicity we spread to our children can be averted in many situations. Yes, it takes time, practice and effort. So if you are not willing to invest in alleviating your defective characteristics, then you will possibly encounter some similar deficiencies in your children. Take the first steps toward action.

We need to identify and acknowledge shortcomings so that we can take action. Having the ability to identify a potential weakness gives us such an advantage. In my estimation, if we identify and acknowledge our problematic areas, then with God's help, we have the opportunity to transform them. Let us visit those two areas of potential growth for our life of influence.

Identify Shortcomings

There are times when we are unwilling, afraid or disinterested in identifying the issues that cause us to abide in being stuck for a long duration. In the long run, unidentified shortcomings can present serious problems. Specifically, you go through life never attending to a wound that could potentially be healed. For example, some people never consider their poor habits, insolence, disrespect, dishonesty or negative attitudes. In many instances, people with that personality or perspective point the finger of blame toward everyone else. In my experience, I have discovered that identifying my shortcomings put me in a position to control my life in a smoother fashion when I combine it with the necessary action from God's word. Shortcomings could be painful and troubling to confront. But the suffering is much worse if the shortcomings remain undefined.

Acknowledge Shortcomings

It is one situation to identify shortcomings, but it is more crucial to acknowledge them as problematic for your life. Anybody can simply point things out. But it is essential to transcend identification and take on accountability. In my opinion, acknowledging shortcomings empowers us to confront circumstances that would otherwise be held against us by other people. Acknowledging our weaknesses can provide us with such a sense of liberty. Releasing ourselves from the incarceration of the mind brings about tremendous benefits. If we are constantly held back regarding our calling, destination or character, we will remain stagnate and precarious about life. Certainly, we are in no position to be strong leaders for our sons with these inhibitions and impediments controlling our minds. We may have a multitude of issues to repair, but we can make strides after acknowledging shortcomings. Why do some men fear or refuse to acknowledge their struggles? Of course, each situation requires adequate time and understanding to address specific matters. But let us look at some of the factors that some fathers may identify as difficult areas.

For many fathers, there is a feeling of vulnerability after acknowledging a struggle. I do not know too many men ecstatic about feeling insecure. I know it is not the highlight of my life. Instead of experiencing vulnerability, many men would rather shut down and let the situation pass. Do not forget our sons are learning behaviors produced and exhibited by us.

It is imperative to work diligently for the proper results and to ultimately defeat the fear that perpetuates stagnation and misinformation to our sons. Patience is primary. Allow me to use a baseball analogy. Stop attempting to hit the home run without investing in the base to base requirements. Acknowledging flaws does have its drawbacks and benefits. But the latter supersedes any potential drawbacks. What influence are you establishing through your ability or inability to acknowledge shortcomings?

Once we have identified and acknowledged our fatherly impediments, life can move forward more smoothly. Your personal accountability list will vary contingent on your circumstances and life voyage. As fathers, feel free to use all the essential steps for reaching your goals in this lifelong journey. My choice of identification and acknowledgement is personal and gives meaning to me.

Make it identifiable, feasible and relevant for your life. But there is one step no father can eliminate. The most vital step for any father is to take action. I will discuss the significance of action in the next chapter. Without action, we are bound to words and dreams that may never come to reality. How do we take action? I really trust when God gives us the direction, we should make the choice to respond accordingly. Stop depending on yourself and surrender to the Lord's power in your life. It really works. I implore you to allow Jesus to influence every step and action. The choice is in our hands. Choose prudently. There is no time to waste.

In my observation and experience, insecurities are often hidden, because they have such a negative connotation. We waste so much time attempting to hide from a situation, it usually forces us to live a life of fantasy. If we do not deal with insecurities, then we unintentionally pass them on. I do highly recommend men to share information in a judicious manner with only those people who are trustworthy and qualified to guide them. Then men are in a position to live unashamed of former faults and misdeeds while willing to take ownership simultaneously.

Address Procrastination

How do we teach our sons the value of being efficient if we have not yet mastered it? Let me give you a reminder. After conquering a fault in our lives, we still should be vigilant not to succumb to ignorance, oversimplification, an ostentatious mindset and false security. Procrastination continues to be a thorn in both of my sides. In many instances, J.D. was the recipient of my unpredictable ways due to my poor habit of procrastination. I must acknowledge my shortcoming of not being effective in a timely manner consistently. I'm guilty. I'm guilty of overloading my responsibilities without always having a solid plan. As a result, I have been negligent with accomplishing important goals. It is unintelligent and counterproductive to be well intentioned and not follow through in an effective manner. In the past, my willingness to procrastinate inhibited me from influencing at the highest level. If we are not reliable with our word, distrust can enter into the most precious relationships. Regaining trust in some circumstances could be an uphill and potentially futile battle. Do not allow your inefficient practices or meaningless words to interfere with the magnitude of your influence. Plan wisely! Be earnest! Think! Act!

Name Your Desires

And be not conformed to this world: but be ye transformed by the renewing of your mind, that ye may prove what is that good, and acceptable, and perfect, will of God (Romans 12:2). Your desires will be instructive, constructive or destructive. You may potentially engage in all three areas involving the influence of your son. For a long duration, I did not take heed or understand thoroughly the significance of a father's desires in relation to the influence with our sons. A father's desires matter enormously. The appropriate desire can manifest a sound outcome for our sons in multiple scenarios. Conversely, inappropriate desires could create dire circumstances, infelicitous behaviors and repulsive actions from our sons. What are your desires as a father? This section deserves enormous attention from us, especially as husbands and family men. But I will get straight to the point. The desires in your life are capable of destroying the wholeness of your family. I strongly encourage you to be vigilant over the desires that masquerade around undetected and thrive in a perpetual indistinguishable disguise. The desires are not just the major concerns, such as adultery, lust, hate and violence. We benefit from recognizing the private and seemingly mundane desires that continue to harm us in subtle ways. The enemy of our soul seeks to destroy us by any measures. Be transparent with God regarding this pursuit. Take time to monitor this very critical life area. Our desires may become the desires of our son.

Identify Your Expectations

Be careful of what you expect from others and your need to control others in subtle or overt ways. It is an extremely thin line between expectations of people and controlling people. It is imperative to provide good judgment, so we do not impose on the lives of others with our unfair expectations. As fathers, we can become controlling and inflexible. Conversely, we can be forgiving and approachable. I encourage you to develop a personal negative and positive influence and expectation list that gives meaning to you regarding your father and son journey.

Negative list

Controlling

What does it mean to be controlling? It means we are putting our thoughts, lives, emotions and welfare before others. I imagine controlling impulses could be done without malice intent. However, it could still be harmful to others when we do not use discernment. I often mention that I do not want to control my children, and I frequently make efforts not to fall into the trap of being a controlling father. But there are certainly times when my authority as a father must be harnessed to avert disconnect and poor communication with my children.

Inflexibility

Are you inflexible in your dealings with your son? Be extremely careful not to give a hasty answer denying a potential problematic area in your father and son rapport. What does being inflexible mean relating to our sons? In some ways, it describes being so obstinate, macho and egotistical that we lose our ability to become highly effective, productive and meaningful fathers.

Positive list

Forgiveness
My non-biological father, Chester, was a forgiving and family engaged man. He had flaws like all fathers but his demeanor toward others taught me valuable lessons. In particular, he reminded me that my biological father loves me, and I will always be grateful for those words. He never met my biological father, but he imparted those words to me at an important time in my life. As fathers, our willingness to forgive and move forward will potentially give meaning to our son's decisive action to forgive. Teach forgiveness for the sake of your son, despite the past challenges and errors of fathers, stepfathers and other men.

I must mention a friend, Greg of more than 20 years who also encouraged me to forgive during some difficult and trying times. When I was 19, he urged me to listen to a song that catapulted me above my heartache and lamenting. It was a beautiful song by a non-popular artist, but it enveloped my heart and set the stage for better communication as a young man seeking to understand life. Allow your willingness to forgive others to remind you that you also have been forgiven.

Be Approachable
How approachable are you? Your answer will partly be based on the way others perceive you. My connection and rapport with young men is contingent on ongoing growth as a listener and a non-judgmental approach. I purposely attempt to learn more from others as opposed to thinking I must be the one always teaching. It is the reciprocal impact that motivates me. Reciprocity keeps the dialog profound, renewed, fair, informative and educational. This is

just my style, and you may have a distinct way of working with people. This is not a matter of one technique being better than another.

Our success in life is inextricably linked to various factors and conditions. Being approachable is not only a skill but an opportunity to rid ourselves of poor habits and build new productive habits. I do believe it takes a measure of honesty to go from unapproachable to approachable standards, especially as a father. Ego will often creep in during the most turbulent, toxic and distracting events within family life. We benefit from getting out of the way of ourselves to become unselfish encouragers of others.

CHAPTER 4

* * *

The Benefit of Sacrificing Fathers and Other Important Factors

Use Accouterments

Are you equipped to do the job of an influencing father? Yes indeed. Now you need to know whether your influence is destructive or productive. In fact, we all have both characteristics in us. Even the Father of the Year needs to work on something despite his stellar record and reputation as a quality father. During the past several years, I could identify with both well-prepared and ill-equipped facets as a father and leader to J.D. I will only concentrate on two important fatherly accouterments (discipline, father and son prayer) while spending quality time and developing a strengthened rapport with my son. Do not forget to take time developing and understanding your personal list for success and challenges regarding your fatherly qualities.

Employ Discipline

What is the first thing that comes to your mind regarding a father that disciplines his child? Most people from the "old school" might make the presumption that it is a father physically beating his children with a belt, switch, hand or all three methods. Of course, many fathers and mothers from back in the day were literally hands-on with their discipline. You could debate whether this was effective or ineffective for you growing up. I will just add this one statement from old school parents. "You will appreciate this beating when you get older." If you can relate to something similar, just smile. In addition, I give my mother so much credit for sticking to her word in an uncompromising fashion. When she put me on restriction, I was not able to go outside no matter the circumstances. If there was a basketball game, friends or the president of the United States visiting my community, then I would miss the event. No questions asked, it was a given that I would be quarantined to the bedroom. Her influence continues to stay with me while raising my children.

In my opinion, true discipline puts me in a position to connect with J.D. on a higher level of respect, love and accountability to God while raising him with the proper standards. It takes an enormous level of patience, teaching, re-teaching, trust, self-control and thinking to avoid doing the first thing that comes to mind. Over these brief years with J.D., I find myself making necessary changes to enhance my ability and actions as a disciplining father. Using scripture to guide my fatherly responses is imperative for current and future success. We do not have all the answers as fathers. Therefore, trusting exclusively on our own self-discipline and self-control will never be adequate for understanding the whole picture. When adhering to our own rules and guidelines, family maladies and malfunctions could soon ensue. I'm grateful for God's word concerning spiritual discipline. Many fathers will decry some of their past errors and pursue a second chance that God provides us.

There are times when I have to walk away, eliminate harmful emotions and grapple with handling tough situations. All husbands are voluntarily signed up for the difficult tasks with confronting issues in family life. God has wired us to handle these situations. Do we always utilize his wisdom within us? Not all the time. Yet I enjoy many flourishing moments while consistently raising J.D. with important values as a stay-at-home father. My contention is not to express that all fathers must stay at home for the best results with their sons. It happens to work for me and my wife. I also trust that a father can stay at home with his son and be an ineffective influence. However, some of the worse father and children predicaments have been transformed. Do not give up. Learning effective influences with J.D. continues to be powerful and useful daily.

I absolutely benefit from raising him in a non-physical manner. I have ascertained his willingness to unconditionally trust Daddy, listen attentively and depend on me to do the right thing. In addition, verbal and emotional abuse could be equally detrimental in our father and son rapport. So your disciplining words should leave the door open for your children to grow, honor, respect and maintain the ability to converse with them in an informed and trustworthy fashion. Honest communication means parents are receptive to listening attentively to some unflattering comments from our children in a respectful manner. In my assessment, there are many times parents succumb to physical discipline due to a lack of self-restraint. In some cases, we have no more tolerance within us. Seriously consider your reason for physical discipline. I'm not attempting to debate parenting methods but to assist us in thinking about the most effective methods while honoring our children. We all benefit from an effective plan when reaching the apex of our frustration. In fact, the better plan for me is to alleviate coming close to that heightened sense of emotional instability.

When disciplining (not physically) my children, I have reminded them of my willingness to hear their side and not shut them out and inundate them with my imposing will, which is not always easy. As a result, my children typically have some questions or further communication even during problematic situations. When disciplining with an open ear, you may find that the Lord desires some parental modifications in your style. There are too many times as parents we concentrate on being correct rather than teaching valuable life lessons. If we are unprepared to teach in a suitable manner, then our children will potentially suppress their genuine thoughts and feelings. Words are spontaneous and retracting them from mid-air is not an option. Once you express harmful words, the lingering impact of those words can be devastating. However, let us not torment ourselves for past errors; we need to be willing to self-examine and earnestly honor our children to avoid harmful parenting techniques. Keep studying His word and trusting the Lord daily for your parent and child influence. Action defeats words! Put your loving words to work by applying them regularly in your parenting duties.

There is nothing like hearing my three-year-old son asks me, "Daddy, how was your day?" Also, my other favorite question is, "Daddy, are you doing okay?" Hearing those questions subsequent to a difficult night will always make it all right. Consequently, I have come to rely on J.D. rushing to the top of the steps every night to greet me with those familiar endearing words. He usually looks me in the eyes and waits for me to pick him up with the response of "My day was fine, and I'm doing great." I'm still learning many of the details as a father. There are so many experiences that I have not encountered at this point like other seasoned fathers. Nevertheless, I look at disciplining J.D. as an ongoing effort toward establishing his outlook, confidence, trust and respect regarding my authority over his life. In addition, I'm setting him up with empowering standards so that he will properly influence the next generation of J.D.s. Any good thing accomplished in my fatherly pursuit was only possible because of the Lord's mercy, loving kindness, grace and word. I could never muster the strength personally to reach a standard of discipline without the Lord's correction in my life. My dependence on the leading of the Holy Ghost will always teach me the relevant fatherly actions.

Father and Son Prayer

"Daddy, give me your hand." "Why, Son?" "I want to pray." I remember getting ready to rush out of the house to work with the young guys before my son chased me down the stairs with those words. He became so in tuned with our normal prayer time together that he did not want me to forget praying with him before exiting the house. He already had a prayer request in mind, and he wanted me to include it in the prayer. Unfortunately, a young boy was badly injured in Washington D.C. from violence in the community. J.D. interrupted my prayer and reminded me to pray for the little boy. He usually specifies his prayer request when he knows people are sick or in need of prayer. I know we often say thank God for a praying grandmother, but I also thank God for a praying son. One of the great things about praying with J.D. continues to be his willingness to pray along with the person praying. He often says "yes" throughout prayer time with Daddy, and it encourages me to keep praying. My wife and I do not say "yes" when we are praying. Where did he get that from? He has a special way of invoking God's presence in his three-year-old style. I have truly learned from J.D. that influence means to have courage and refuse to be ashamed of your relationship with Jesus.

Select True Mentors

I usually tell my young mentees about the importance of mentors in my life. I do have several men in my life with more wisdom, experience and a relationship with the Lord that assist me in significant life areas. The most important focus points in my life are God, family and young people. These men are willing to speak candidly with me about my faults and encourage me with moving forward in those pivotal areas. The truth really does set you free. They teach ways to identify things which make me successful and ways to pursue pertinent goals. In fact, I could never reach a level of enduring success with young men unless I was able to address personal shortcomings that have been pointed out, corrected and guided in the proper path by my mentors. It certainly makes a difference when men in authority are willing to uplift you with the truth about your life in a respectful fashion. Mentors encourage other mentors. However, I highly recommend taking the adequate time to select a mentor that practices the things that they speak. I can really say that I have encountered and benefited from positive men in my life. But mentors who live in integrity are precious gems, and their value is unmatched. The influence of godly men propels the life of all men willing to practice beneficial family methods.

Enact a Reward System

J.D. will try extra hard at completing tasks when he knows there is something to look forward to as a reward. The ability to influence through a reward system with J.D. proves to be successful with the proper principles and teaching in place. His mind responds differently when he knows that he will earn something for giving effort. There are certainly factors in determining the best times to reward and when to avoid conveying the wrong message to him. I think there can be a fine line between rewarding children and manipulating them to do the right thing. So I typically reward J.D. when I think he can benefit from an incentive to give additional effort. The reward does not need to be tangible, but you can utilize whatever things are relevant for your child's motivation.

However, I'm mindful of not attempting to trick him into doing something because I lack doing my job as a parent. This is not to make any parents feel discouraged when you are having a tough day and just fall short as a parent. Most of us have those days. Truthfully, I find myself having to convince myself to not take the easy route of parenting from time to time. (J.D. would say, "hard work-work"). I would rather work intelligently, diligently, honestly and prayerfully to communicate the proper message to him. But I also notice that even when I have tough days in parenting the investment of being consistent with J.D. pays *dividends*. The ability to remain trustworthy among our sons conveys a message of influence by default. You will not always need to give a gift, goodie or gadget, but the actions of a loving father will reward him sufficiently. Thanks, Father God, for first showing me ways to reward J.D. through love.

Show Acumen as a Parent

Being judicious and keen as a parent will be meaningful in your decision making. How many times have you said "yes" when the answer should be "no"? Join the crowd. However, inconsistency, ineptitude and improper methods are also (negative) influential tools. Unfortunately, they are the tools that put our parenting values into questionable categories. What resources do you use to develop parenting acumen? The values, love, perspectives, wisdom, insight and experience are some of the important factors regarding raising our children. Consider your personal parenting acumen list. Ultimately, we benefit from increasing parenting wisdom and not depending on our children to just figure it out. Our ability to influence effectively depends on growing in our virtues, insight, love and discipline throughout the parenting journey.

I enjoy hearing people say, "There is no handbook for parenting." However, I think we have access to the greatest parenting handbook in God's word. The reality is having access to the greatest resource without application will still leave us stuck. Some of the parenting tools, such as patience, truth, knowledge, love and compassion, are valuable in our daily connection with our children. However, the ability to effectively influence is not only a matter of our parenting acumen but also sincerely making strides at dealing with our parenting deficiencies. In too many circumstances, there is non-commitment toward identifying the personal errors in parenting.

Parents will need to be careful not to encourage their children with ill-informed, ill-equipped and ill-suited verbalizations or behaviors in all environments. Be cognizant of blaming others and influencing your children consistently with dishonest approaches. Trust me! They are absolutely observant and take in the action. Oftentimes children know the truth, but they are hijacked by the lack of standards displayed by parents. I was at a car dealership in October 2014 and a mother of five began conversing with me about competitive parents who consistently blame others for their children's issues, errors, flaws and mistakes, in other words, parents instilling unaccountable thoughts in the minds of their children without any hesitation. It will certainly be counterproductive and harmful for the long duration. Realistically, we all must be aware of trapping our children with disruptive and limited thinking. When we attempt to make our children feel secure while neglecting the importance of responsibility, then we are doing them a disservice. Sound familiar? If it does reflect you and your parenting style, it is not too late to rectify it.

I want to reflect on the teacher–student relationship throughout many of our schools. But before addressing the teacher and student dynamics, allow me to make an observation. I will preface my statement by mentioning the portrayal of some teachers in the news behaving in insidious ways and engaging in infelicitous relationships. However, these types of relationships have not only been limited to teachers. Parents, counselors, mentors, coaches, politicians, police officers and other leaders are accountable for many problematic interactions with our children. These horrible situations have occurred more times than I care to think about. It will be paramount for us to enhance the trustworthiness of our leaders among young people to help us regain the proper relationships. We all know social media preserves misdeeds and spreads the horrific actions at the speed of touching a button. So we have a copious amount of destructive issues to overcome and important resolutions to identify.

Now, let me address the teacher and student rapport. There are some great teachers in our schools, and I have come across many of them. As parents, many of us can identify some positive factors regarding relationships among teachers, parents and students. I also observed some reasons for negative actions from students primarily due to parents conveying mixed messages in front of their children. Nobody wants to hear negative things about their children from a teacher or anybody else. But we must also be willing to confront the truth when our children behave with malfeasance, disrespect or inappropriate actions. So avoid communicating irresponsible behavior to your children because it could potentially restrict their life growth in various areas. I strongly suggest alleviating negative discussions in front of your children when you are averse to a teacher's methods in the classroom. I often tell my youngest daughter (second grader) that teachers are to be respected, and we can appropriately address any situations of disagreement at home. I'm extremely grateful for several years of consistent positive reports from teachers regarding Azaria's interactions with peers and teachers.

When I grew up in Philly, teachers had the liberty to confront the misdeeds of students without fear of ramifications from parents. I would not even consider coming home telling my mother about how terrible the teacher was at school. It was not an option unless I wanted to get into more trouble. Truthfully, I was not a consistent model student in school. It was most definitely best for me to keep silent about any negative thoughts concerning teachers being mean. Although my academic situation was relatively good, I give credit to many of the committed teachers during my youthful years.

I recognize we now are dealing with a new generation, but there are some traditional methods that have long-lasting appeal in my influencing tools. Respect, strong work ethics, prayer and compassion will never lose their potency. My mother encouraged her children to attend school regularly through her model work practices. We were motivated to attend school even during inclement weather, and we received perfect attendance records annually throughout our school years. What do you think is the major obstruction regarding the seemingly faltering teacher, parent and student rapport? We do not need to debate, but it is worth reflecting on your sense of the disconnection with teachers, students and parents. There are times when parents may be justified in their assessment with specific teachers. But it is critically important to completely alleviate your harmful thoughts about the teacher in front of your children. I promise you that they feed off the negative energy, and it only fuels the fire to bring additional conflict with the teacher. As parents, it is imperative to self-examine and earnestly work through your shortcomings to eliminate the certainty of passing on the wrong message to our children. In short, deal with you. I would be remiss by not adding the necessity to seek the Lord's truth and wisdom for correcting your errors in parenting. It *absolutely* makes a difference with effective influencing among your children and their interactions with their teachers. I'm not exempt from providing the right example, and it is so clear that leadership begins with the parent.

Honor a Sacrificing Wife

It can be difficult spending quality time consistently with my wife due to our schedules. We continue to find creative ways to enjoy productive time together. I stay at home with our son (and daughter when she comes home from school). When my wife returns home from work, then I leave to go to work with the young people. On the weekends, we reverse our roles and I'm typically out of the home most of the day. My wife and I have experienced the scope of not being able to do all the things we desire in our family and personal lives. It means a tremendous amount to have an understanding, committed and loving wife. I give my bride credit for being a sacrificing family woman and not putting additional pressure and stress on our marriage. In addition, the sacrifices from my wife continue to put us in a position to flourish and enhance our married life.

We have been able to improve our communication, resources, love, respect and patience throughout this marriage voyage. However, we never claim that we have arrived at the culmination of our relationship. I think it can be dangerous to claim total victory and complete conquering regarding all family challenges. But we continue to grow in our understanding of the principle of being one in marriage. *Therefore a man shall leave his father and his mother and shall become united and cleave to his wife, and they shall become one flesh (Genesis 2:24).*

If you have a sacrificing wife, continue to love, encourage and motivate her without boundaries. She deserves it completely, and it will not go unnoticed when done with care. The influence of a sacrificing, godly and understanding wife continues to assist with the balance of my household. Nevertheless, the husband should be prepared to lead his household with love, integrity, peace, strength and spiritual discipline. Therefore, I do not allow the aforementioned complicated schedule with my wife to overwhelm me. I encourage you to always persevere and constantly maintain your fortitude in this marriage journey. May every husband abandon selfish motives and pour unconditional love into your sacrificing bride. Appropriately, the influence of the household is tremendously enhanced when husband and wife are partners with similar objectives. *As for me and my house, we will serve the Lord (Joshua 24:15).*

Take Action

Be the revolution. In many cases, fathers will need to become the extraordinary change for our little champions. I can assure you, it will be nearly impossible without taking action. Taking action is such a paramount position for any father. Why? It takes precedence over everything preceding the action. Have you ever made a promise to your son and failed to keep it? Over and over again! We benefit from understanding the mistrust that develops from a lack of action. I did not say we are no longer loved by our sons. The ability to influence through action is contingent on your ability to put your words into practice consistently. Being a pragmatic father means we should be cognizant of the superfluous words being disseminated toward our sons. We have all been negligent by not moving forward with action. I encourage us to not make unreliable words a normal practice and influence in our rapport with children.

However, I sometimes ponder on the many things we take for granted without considering the major impact on our sons. Do you ever consider the impact of dishonest living in front of your children? What about the impact of compromising your values? How about the way you handle obstacles in front of your son? Are you a shut-down father? Do you demonstrate aggressiveness? Are your children fearful of you? The ability or inability to influence properly will manifest at home, school or in the community—possibly all three places! Yet it is not too late to regain your rightful place in the home as an action-oriented husband. Realistically, it is consistent work from fathers that will empower the next generation of young men. I absolutely notice the trust and obedience from J.D. increase when my actions are aligned with my words. J.D.'s actions have a direct correlation with the conduct I demonstrate in life.

Think in a transcendent fashion, but more important, take action in a transcendent manner. In other words, planning ahead is vital, but execution of our plans should be essential. Notice the copious amount of times we say things loosely without an intention of fulfilling our words with our sons. I do not know about you, but I have caught myself doing this more times than I care to share. There are many reasons for this misleading, such as being preoccupied, negligent, careless or inattentive to the significance of saying what you mean and performing it. In my experience, the small things matter concerning keeping my word and taking action with J.D.

It means something for him when I take action with pouring him a glass of milk, reading a book, watching cartoons and simply paying attention to the father and son connection. Action only means you are willing to follow through with what you mentioned doing concerning the father and son influence. The word that needs emphasis is "you." It does require a high level of discipline, integrity and growth to engage in the mundane father and son activities. New fathers, I encourage you to take your time and do not give into self-defeat when encountering errors. Allow yourself to learn the hope acquired through accomplishing the small things with your son. It is a big deal! The smaller the event with your son requires greater action from Dad. Think small to achieve big with your son.

DIT: Daddy In Training

Currently, I label myself as a daddy in training, although I have 18 years of experience as a father. I'm not a new pup in the fatherhood business. But I need to continue learning and working on enhancing my fatherly skills. I also believe retreating from training as a father makes us vulnerable to additional errors and opens us up to a false sense of mastery. Once we master a skill, we benefit from making strides in other areas where we are less proficient. So I'm still a daddy in training (DIT) for now, because I have a substantial way to go before reaching the best results with my son. I do not only want to affect J.D. and leave the rest of the young men behind. There are many young men who need to see fathers unified in order to transform much of the toxicity ahead of them. What toxicity? I don't know where to start. Take your pick! However, many of our young men are being trained to become poor leaders and fathers from too many unqualified sources. Teaching our sons to continue in a path of self-loathing, immorality, violence and abuse are some of the disqualifying factors. Even with that being the case, I'm still not disheartened. So I'm implying that men must take a stand in helping our sons arise from a bleak future. It starts with me and you, brother. Being a daddy in training primarily means you are willing to continue prospering for the betterment of all sons and daughters.

Delve Beneath the Surface of the Father and Son Influence

J.D. is only three years old, and I have not even begun to scratch the surface regarding our father and son influence. I'm at the planting stage with him. The next step will be the watering stage. The phenomenal thing about both stages is God gives the increase. *I have planted, Apollos watered; but God gave the increase (1 Corinthians 3:6).* I have not even begun to get heated up about our future together. In other words, the best is still ahead of us, and reaching toward that point continues to be extremely inspiring. What do we have to look forward to in this voyage? Plenty!

Over the next year, I will remain at home with him as our bond develops. In that scope of time, we will learn more about one another, especially with his ever-developing personality. The next year will demand focus and attention from me as I prepare him for kindergarten. I'm sure it will feel great to send him off to school with all the other children. Did I mention that it will be amazing experiencing a break during the daytime? Yes, I will enjoy getting up in the morning and focusing more on my youth agency without so many interruptions. J.D.'s interruptions have no limits. "Daddy, can you fix my game?" "Can you give me a snack?" "Are you ready to go outside?" "Can I feed the fish?" "What time is it?" "Daddy, come here and watch this!" "Daddy!" "Daddy!" I have not even scratched the surface with his desire to connect with Daddy at some of the most inconvenient times. Smile, Dad! You do not have to be a stay-at-home father to relate to putting everything down for the sake of your child. Even though many of us are overwhelmed with tremendously busy schedules, influence requires sacrifice. As fathers, the ability to exhibit unselfishness, trustworthiness and commitment delivers auspicious results for our father and son influence. Like father, like son!

Do I want my son to replicate me? I have come to the understanding that the most important quality about any individual is being an authentic you. Some parents attempt to live through the experiences of their children. There is no need to feel disheartened about it, but we certainly should be aware of poor parenting techniques. I sometimes witness vicarious living of children with the reality shows on cable. What are your aspirations for your son? I can honestly say there are so many things that I would never want my son to duplicate from my life. But he will still make his own life errors. People say that it is important to learn from our errors. I still like to say there is one more step. Take action! When we take action, I trust we become more equipped in our credibility, purpose and service to others.

Of course, there are certainly qualities that I think J.D. will naturally pick up from me. What qualities would Daddy like to pass on? I want to consistently symbolize trustworthiness, commitment, athleticism, hard work-work (J.D.'s theme), serious-minded focus, reflective thinking, influencing, loving, being peaceful, competing, being dedicated, forgiving, health conscious, tenacious, hope-filled and a lover of Jesus Christ above everything else mentioned. Yes, that is just the initial attributes I aspire to pass on to J.D. I do not want to overwhelm you with boredom attempting to complete the list. By the way, I have a longer list of personal errors in life that J.D. and Daddy will cover during our progress within the father and son journey.

What about the teenage years stage? In my work with young men, I'm already getting a glimpse of both sides of the equation. Working with such a diverse population of young men continues to give me an edge regarding things to possibly expect. However, even with the best preparation, I understand circumstances can still devastate and overtake you. In boxing, it is expressed that you do not know how well you will respond until you have been hit and tested. Can you take a punch? You must have good whiskers (metaphor for chin) in order to keep standing when getting hit unexpectedly. Everyone looks good prior to engaging in the heat of the battle. Have you ever listened to people prematurely talk about how tough they are before encountering a difficult situation? In some cases, those individuals break down in fear, tears and retreat when dealing with real life.

So I recognize my greatest advantage is unceasing trust in the Lord. *Lean on, trust in, and be confident in the Lord with all your heart and mind and do not rely on your own insight or understanding (Proverbs 3:5).* I'm no exception. The teenage years with J.D. are far off at this point. When we arrive, it could possibly be a totally different dynamic than what we are encountering today with young people. Influence is not a matter of the age, but it is a matter of the generation Sustainer (Jesus). No time for fear or trepidation! I trust that Daddy will be prepared for the good, bad and middle ground regarding the next 10 years. What about the impending stages?

Who do I think J.D. will become as an adult? Well, I will not entertain my own question too deeply, because I will disclose subjective answers. What did you think I would say? He is my son. Smile! So I trust he will become many great things in his journey, and I believe his impact will influence my life tremendously. It seems to constantly revolve back to the reciprocal influence. My vision for J.D. will never be an adequate description, because I'm limited in my perspective of what God has for his life. But I do tell him frequently in his ear that he will become a great influencer among people. He usually responds in the affirmative. I told you my answer would be subjective. Mostly, it is between J.D. and the Lord. I'm just his teacher attempting to give him some good lessons along the way. We both will need to look up to our Father in heaven for the proper guidance.

CHAPTER 5

————— * * * —————

Teach Your Son to Become an Exemplary Man

Strive for Quality Time versus Time

HAVE YOU EVER juxtaposed being available against being accessible? It is a difference between being available as a father and making yourself accessible. The major differences will determine the outcome of your influence in the father and son relationship. I'm implying being accessible enables greater rewards than simply being available. Fathers may not take the time to distinguish the important factors between being available and accessible. But understanding the meticulous components within these two areas delivers strategic results each father needs with his son. Is it possible to provide quality time (accessibility) on a consistent basis? Yes indeed. As fathers, we need to figure out what our sons need during quality time. More important, learn ways to make quality time a reciprocal experience. Fathers should benefit just as much as sons during your accessible moments. It can sustain the authenticity in your connection with your son. Let us take time to dissect the two thoughts regarding availability and accessibility within the father and son rapport.

Availability is not a terrible thing regarding our father and son influence. However, I consider it the foundation for developing a more intimate meaning and purpose with our sons. As a father, being available is certainly an intricate piece to raising our sons and providing a sense of security for them. During the availability moments, we can glean vital information from our sons that can be used during the accessibility times. In my assessment of J.D., availability enables me to build on security, trust, courage and dependability along with other important factors for both father and son.

As fathers, being there (availability) is an essential tool for learning ways to deepen, strengthen and activate every attainable goal for the father and son influence. I urge fathers to initiate their availability and seek the wisdom of God to become compelled to transcend this basic stage with your son. Let me impart one additional encouragement. It is never too late for fathers to recognize and then become available to our sons. Your human frailties will try to persuade you to give up. We can frequently be our worse enemies in this journey of reparation with our children. But it is critical to keep making progress. Subsequent to becoming a consistently available father, I trust your ability to become accessible will take over. Of course, we should be sincere during each level of the father and son influence.

It does not mean we are perfect fathers because we become an accessible father. Accessibility does not characterize the father and son influence, but it develops and molds it into something special. Accessibility is the stage of investment in our son's creative, imaginative, and pragmatic involvement with life. His worldview takes precedence above the things fathers inspire their sons to become in life. Get out of the way, Dad! Accessibility is the place fathers guide and not enforce and impose their standards on their sons. How effective are you as an accessible father?

I should acknowledge the definition of an accessible father was birthed from my understanding of the mistakes incurred during playtime with J.D. During recreational time with J.D., he frequently had a plan for me and him. It typically required me to listen to his instructions and adhere to his commands regarding each game. He was not satisfied with playing basketball the conventional way. I had to stand a specific way and play defense according to his guidelines. He had particular instructions that were premeditated, enforced and necessary in each activity for the day.

Playing with his race cars on the floor requires meticulous attention to speed, distance and a skill to crash at the perfect point of destruction. Do you get the point? The ability to influence must first satisfy the prerequisite of being influenced in some of the most elementary games with your son. It matters to him whether you are committed to allowing him to initiate the rules, make adjustments, delegate and deliver the conclusion of the games. If your son is anything like J.D., it may take a great deal of time before the game reaches a conclusion. Fathers may need to modify when the game will actually come to an end. Smile, it is okay. When you become accessible to your son, quality time supersedes merely spending time with him.

During the accessible plateau, there is no right or wrong way. Just be there and surrender to the fun standards and plans our sons have laid out for us. Can you see the total picture? It starts with becoming available, then navigating your way to accessible. His worldview is what really matters.

Encourage Relationships with Other Men

I really believe that sending perplexing messages is a very dangerous idea regarding the development of our sons' characters. If we are one way with one set of friends and exhibit contradicting behavior with a different group of friends, then we will probably lose some respect from our sons. They will not tell us, but it will be their experience of double-minded actions from us. I'm describing the tendency to live in hypocrisy instead of being firmly fixed in character. People pleasing will never allow you to rest. It will cause you to vacillate in your character and distort your true identity. Although I'm serious natured, I really enjoy considering the feelings of others. Therefore, I continue to benefit from working on speaking the truth in love. In addition, our sons are like sponges, and the things you undervalue in actions could be detrimental toward them. Also, I have come to learn that your true friends will value, respect, appreciate and become influenced when your lifestyle exhibits integrity.

I want my son to know all of my friends and allow him to form his own thoughts and discuss them with his daddy. I realize we are not able to guard our sons from every negative person or situation. In fact, I like to utilize those situations as powerful teaching moments. In addition, I do not attempt to make people live, think or respond according to my standards. Therefore, my message to J.D. regarding my friendships with other men will hopefully convey respect, peace and trustworthiness.

Respect Relationships with Other Women

Every person has his or her individual thoughts regarding interactions with the opposite sex. Some people believe that married people should not have friends of the opposite sex, and others think it is fine. What do you think?

You have to know, respect and communicate with your spouse about this sensitive matter. If we are not serious enough with taking the time to make wise decisions in this area, then it could create marital and family destruction. I'm not giving premarital counseling or marriage counseling advice, but I'm implying proper relationships with the opposite sex are worth investing time in thorough dialog with your bride or groom. Although the enemy desires to crush families, we should also consider our responsibility in our foundational and ongoing relationships.

What do I want J.D. to take away from my relationship with other women? First, I want him to understand through my actions that my bride has precedence over any working relationship or friendship with the opposite sex. Second, I'm so grateful that my wife reminds me of her deep trust and security because of my fidelity in marriage. Now, all I have to do is work on all those other deficiencies! Smile. My wife and I will constantly have some area to enhance in our marriage and family life journey. There are many husbands who really do ensure that they protect, guard and avoid causing harm to their wives regarding infidelity. Personally, it feels good to know quite a few awesome husbands and family men. I truly believe this is an enormous advantage, especially for our sons regarding family values, spousal commitment and marriage endurance.

Be Careful to Limit Self-trust

I think many people have an illusion about how Christians sustain their success. But I want to personally mention some important facts for my life. I do feel focused, disciplined, intelligent and courageous when trusting the Lord. In addition, I do acknowledge having additional attributes dispensed by the Lord. My contention for the ongoing personal success continues to be a desire to adhere to the Lord's word. I certainly have flaws in my life too. You may argue that it takes certain attributes to surrender to God's word. Well, we can go back and forth with that point. There is too much to communicate without me getting off course with my main idea. However, I recognize that when God is directing me, it is up to me to choose obedience. Whenever I yield to His will, the Holy Spirit directs me further.

For example, the Holy Spirit directed me as a young man on ways to avoid trapping myself in an ongoing promiscuous lifestyle. I began avoiding one-on-one time with females and the temptation that came with it. It was a simple resolution. Here is the biggest question. Are you willing to submit to God's influence for your peace? In my opinion, this is one of the biggest difference makers between those who struggle with living in peace and those who adorn their lives in peace. I will give one more example.

Unfortunately, there are so many people trapped in sexual immorality through cable and social media without using simple resolutions that God desires for your life. I will insert a quick thought before addressing this next example. There is no greater influence in my life superseding the power of God. As a result, my ability to remain a responsible influencer to J.D. will unceasingly reside in my reliance on the Spirit of God. In addition, I'm grateful for ongoing endeavors regarding a strong level of discipline, trustworthiness, self-control and other qualities. In reality, those attributes are a result of conscious work in my spiritually disciplined life and His grace. We benefit from understanding what qualities need to be inserted in our character. But your attributes reduce their magnitude of impact without a total dependence on the presence of God. Therefore, influencing our sons and other young men depends on being influenced by His power, especially when real life issues come our way.

Now, my next example deals with what people put in their minds and hearts. I constantly guard and communicate about what my children are exposed to in my home. If we just shut down without healthy dialog, it may become an opening for rebellious actions from our children. It really helps when I can discuss anything with my children in order to appropriately influence them. I'm open to talking about life, school, sports, relationships, problems, friends, animals and anything my children can imagine. If not me, then who will talk about it? Possibly the wrong person!

There are too many events our children are witnessing in our homes without the protection of parents. Allow me to dig deeper regarding our ability to guard our children inside our homes. I have not even touched on what they will come in contact with outside our home. But all types of influence will reveal itself in subtle ways.

I did not recognize the influential power regarding television, especially as an adolescent. Now, I absolutely have God's wisdom to understand it in a proficient manner. Children are not the only ones being submerged into a life of immoral thoughts and living. I vividly recognized the danger of having specific cable channels in our home several years ago. I understand there are some devices to assist in not allowing our children to be exposed to some of the lascivious material. But I'm not concentrating on the children. I'm confronting what influences us as the leaders of our homes. What prevents you from becoming victimized by the immoral influences?

Some of the commercials alone can be so obscene that even the most spiritually disciplined person can be tripped up. My main point is I do not put too much trust in myself. When it is clear that God is showing me the things I need to avoid, then it is worthwhile for me to make the right choice based on His word. Trust me, friend, we all are susceptible to slip-ups and giving into sin. One of the greatest allies to counterattack the self-trust mode continues to be my yielding to God's way of escape. If I spend too much time contemplating, then it could result into increasing my desire to become engrossed into temptation. No time for that! Being action oriented with His word proves to be successful for me in optimizing beneficial outcomes. So I continue to express that I'm not so strong. Realistically, I do not have to be too strong. Instead I would rather yield to His guidance, so I can confront the temptation. Make no mistake about it! Your children to some extent are only as good as the influence within you. Too much self-trust can convert itself into self-deception.

Engage in the Crucibles and Quagmires of Life

If we think we can completely avoid the severe tests and difficulties of life, then we are tricking ourselves. I think it is highly irresponsible to define a person based on whether they failed handling an obstacle in life. We all have bad days, and there are times when we display negativity toward others. It does not mean that we must now be encompassed or entrapped by that error for the rest of our lives. Misery does love company, and people who are displeased with their lives would love to drag you through the muddy waters of life. So I enjoy teaching young people that their current problems do not resolve who they will necessarily become in the future.

Learning ways to influence is extremely vital when those you influence do not pursue, seek or understand the value of alternatives in their lives. Similarly, they simply feel completely stuck. If you are an influencer, then remain alert regarding personal crucibles attempting to overtake your thoughts and actions. I have noticed a few times when professionals become intolerant of their clients because the professional did not sufficiently grapple with his or her own personal quagmire. You will influence others commensurate with your internal peace and clarity. The level of education and personal accolades will not substitute for internal fortitude granted by the Lord. There are times when we are leaning on things, people or actions to sustain us, but they have no substance to empower us.

By the way, many clinical counselors, mentors, doctors, teachers, pastors and leaders encounter personal problems frequently. We are human beings, and no person can avoid dealing with life issues. Therefore, it is worthwhile investing in a person to pray with you, encourage you, speak truthfully, provide you with wisdom and be there to confide in as necessary. Conversely, take precaution and use discretion regarding sharing confidential information with just anybody who desires to listen to you. It could certainly come back to burn you by sharing too much. It is important to understand the position and calling over your life. It really is true that it takes many years to build a solid reputation, but it only takes one situation to bring that reputation crashing down. Unfortunately, there are people who enjoy slandering the character of others because of envy, hate, insecurity or self-loathing. Think carefully! Always forgive! The influence of a severe life test should enlighten you to travel a new pathway of self-control, power and a focus on your destination.

Use Social Media Sparingly

Are you spending more time on social media than your children? Be honest about it. How do we ask our children to reduce their time on social media if we are doing the opposite? Where is the integrity? Exemplary men are consistent in their modeling behavior. Notice that I did not say perfect. Also, even if you attempted to put on the façade of perfection, it will backfire. No child can withstand those standards. But there is value in being steadfast in your faith and standards. I have no problem with social media, because it can be utilized in a powerful, effective and connecting manner. However, influence through social media can be counterproductive if we are unwilling to become non-social when merited.

Avoid Ostentation

Do you know people who are show-offs? In some ways, I was out of control with my desire to show off certain skills or try to fit in with the older guys beginning early in my life. Although I did not learn my lesson quickly enough as an ostentatious child, my older cousin, Yvette made me face the repercussions for my misbehaviors. This next situation with my cousin is strictly being mentioned as a humorous story and nothing else.

I was approximately nine years old and my older cousin was in charge of babysitting me. For some reason, I frequently had the tendency of attempting to impress the older guys with my mischievous and outright bad behaviors. I do not recall all the details regarding my behaviors, but my cousin would probably have an assortment of misbehaviors performed by me. She would typically be embarrassed by my behavior, but she had the answer when she got me home. There were no beatings, hitting or abuse done to me. Instead, she would put my curly long hair into braids. In those days, braids were not cool or stylish for little boys. Maybe that is why I enjoy having a bald head today. Just kidding! It is still so interesting that I would do any negative behaviors, so I could get the attention of the older guys. Influence can be a dangerous thing when a young boy is misguided by his own choices, desires and misperceptions.

CHAPTER 6

* * *
Developing Trust

Do You Trust Daddy?

I FREQUENTLY ASK my son this critical question to gauge his emotional connection regarding the father–son relationship. I really feel he depends on me completely to be a trustworthy daddy. J.D. usually answers in the affirmative regarding his trust for me. Trust is such a critical factor for a father, because it carries a substantial amount of weight within the father–son rapport. Trust is enhanced when fathers are good leaders, demonstrate consistency, communicate with purpose, demonstrate humility and love with God's unconditional love. Fathers benefit from gaining their sons' trust through providing the best example for them in every area, not just telling them in words but magnifying those words through actions. I must admit, it is not always easy, but the reward for our sons is priceless. When you ask your son whether he trusts you, be prepared for necessary adjustments for an even deeper level of trust.

Reinforce Influence

One of the helpful reinforcing tactics in which I engage J.D. is to repeat what I'm conveying to him. I'm impressed with what children can discuss with us if we are patient enough to explain to them and listen to their responses. I literally ask J.D. to repeat my words for two reasons. First, I want to ascertain that he understands what I'm saying. Secondly, I prefer to try things that help me to teach accountability with my children. I really think my children appreciate my desire to teach in a humble manner compared to being dogmatic with them. However, there are certainly times when I must restrain my emotions, so I will not cross the line. Reinforcing influence can be done in a multitude of ways. Reinforce through love, correction, guidance, insight, patience, purpose and a mindset to experience self-reinforcement.

Stay Focused From Start to Finish

Are you constantly interrupted from completing tasks? What do you allow to get in the way of finishing goals? Reflect! One of the impediments that I noticed about my life was starting things and not fulfilling their original purpose in a timely manner. This was not only a matter of procrastination but in many cases self-interruption. It could be minor, moderate or major things that were not being fulfilled on my end. I found myself being distracted from simple tasks, such as making up the bed in the morning, to achieving personal goals. In some more important circumstances, it was a matter of not doing my best. By taking notice of my self-interrupting habits, I saw some of the personal poor habits in my life. Habits! Watch habits! They can constitute some serious faulty agendas for your life if they go unchecked. Take the time to watch the interruptions in your life and whether it damages your credibility, influence, integrity and dependability.

There are times when I did not consistently follow through with my children or mentees, as well as personal endeavors. Good intentions are not always sufficient when we lack fulfilling the intended purpose. Starting projects of any kind are great, but the ability to complete them delivers future auspicious results. Vision matters! But let me ask this question. Do you have the guts to believe when the vision is clear, but it requires surviving a severe self-test? You may need to make some serious adjustments in your personal skills. I trust that self-examination will be beneficial for moving beyond this crucible. Unfortunately, there are times when you would rather drench yourself in the success of others instead of following your treasure from God. Watch out for coveting! Trust in the inspiration that was meant specifically for you.

We are more valuable than settling for the residue of others. Therefore, self-influence matters greatly. When we are able to identify, determine, transform, counter and monitor our self-weakness, this becomes advantageous for those relying on our influential service. A greater measure of trust derives from those that see you initiate, concentrate, follow through consistently and care for the best results. Furthermore, if you already established a way to reach your destination continually, then I applaud you for working through the quagmires of life. The willingness to finish what we begin is an enduring value to revel in constantly. Do not allow your influence to be affirmed on false images, dishonorable measures, envy, emptiness and self-illusion. Many people initiate great works. But finishing is more valuable, influential and enduring in most circumstances. *I have glorified You down here on the earth by completing the work that You gave Me to do (John 17:4).*

Choose Options over Limits

I mostly believe there are usually options or alternatives available to us in life in practically every circumstance. In fact, our limits are in some cases predicated on our inability, unwillingness or non-commitment to producing or generating a way out. Why is it vital to assist our sons with utilizing the multitude of options for their lives? It puts them in a position to grapple with life in a more profound way. If you feel caged, then you will probably live, respond and behave in a limited manner.

Being limited should not be an option. But I trust the development, growth and ability of our sons pursuing alternatives effectively will be initiated by fathers who are willing to teach God's wisdom and truth. Unfortunately, all other alternatives leave us with limits. It does not mean we should beat our sons over the head with scripture each moment. I have observed well-intentioned fathers experience counterproductive results due to children not being prepared for the spiritual overload. Each family situation requires unique approaches, but the proper foundation will potentially connect our sons with productive options. In the words of J.D., I will say fathers will need to engage in "hard work-work."

Find Power in a Greeting

When J.D. and I are hanging out in the community, so many people have taken the time to greet him in an affable manner. The greeting usually extends to small talk and some type of compliment toward him. In most instances, he will shy away from talking at length until he warms up to a person. But this does not prevent people from treating him in such a kind way. In particular, every week at church he can depend on a special greeting.

There is a kind lady from the church we attend who constantly meets him at his seat and provides him with a lollipop. She also gave our children some race cars, books and other generous gifts. When speaking to my wife, this woman expressed kind words about our children and their similarity to her own grandchildren. The power of a greeting does not terminate subsequent to departing from an individual's presence, but it delivers a lasting and galvanizing experience. There are so many nice people who simply enjoy smiling and being pleasant to others. I encourage all of us to greet others with the power of a smile, handshake and friendliness. As the saying goes, "It does not cost you anything to be nice."

Teaching J.D. the proper way to greet people is an ongoing assignment. Mostly, he will mimic Daddy's specific greetings and verbalizations witnessed during our outings in the community. I do certain things according to the traditional way. I consider myself "old school" with various styles, although I attempt keeping up with the swag of the young people, which is no easy task for me.

There are essential ways to greet adults and my wife and I do not compromise in these areas. Our children must call all adults either Mr., Mrs. or Ms. when greeting them. No exceptions! In this day and time, I also teach our children ways to hug people in an appropriate manner. You may have your own style. In fact, there is nothing off limits when communicating with our children becoming informed with respectful interaction, approaching politely and greeting adults. It calls for adjustments and there are times when I need to do better at my manners. My daughter, Azaria usually asks good questions, and she is willing to point out my deficiencies in a respectful, humble and caring manner. No problem, Daughter! I really do not mind, because developing the character of our children should not limit appropriate behaviors for the children exclusively.

Remember that Reputation Matters

I assure you that reputation matters when you least expect it to be the case. Even if people do not admit it, we all remember both sides of the reputation coin. We certainly recall individuals who made a negative impression on us through some obscene or irresponsible conduct. Conversely, people exhibiting compassion, kindness and affable behavior are not easily forgotten. Many times, it only takes a friendly smile to make a difference concerning the outcome of a situation. What do you want your reputation to convey about you?

Your reputation, above so many other attributes, puts you in a position to be either an effective or ineffective influencer of young men (and women). Reputation speaks for itself, and it spreads like nothing else. Hopefully, people will judge you on the merits of your reputation. I always recommend checking people out personally, because there are times when individuals mischaracterize others for personal reasons. There are so many horrible stories, especially regarding young people, that circulate on social media, which are blatant lies and reputation destroyers. I encourage you to keep moving forward and do not become consumed with situations that are out of your control. In addition, allow your reputation to be reestablished on what Jesus says about you. Your accusers will no longer have the same control over you. *When Jesus raised Himself up, He said to her, Woman where are your accusers? Has no man condemned you? (John 8:10).*

Primarily, you do not have to boast when you really match up with a reputation of integrity. There is no need to seek attention, because people will be taken in by the accountability of your actions. Also, at all cost, endeavor to avoid the temptation of people pleasing. If you are influencing others with a hidden agenda and unrealistic pursuits, then you have already caused damage to yourself and those depending on you for guidance. Honesty matters! Be willing to self-examine constantly in order to update goals and make pertinent adjustments that align with your purpose. So proceed with confidence, exuberance and a willingness to activate a character that portrays an authentic individual. There are two people who you can never fool in life. You do not need me to tell you the two people, although, I think we attempt to trick ourselves at times. However, the Lord understands our frailties and desires to equip us during our most troubled conditions.

In the beginning, being a stay-at-home father had put me in a precarious situation regarding ways to productively maintain my agency with youths. There were ambivalent thoughts going through my mind. On the one hand, I really wanted to spend an enormous amount of quality time working with young people. On the other hand, I also deeply desired developing a bond with J.D. My final decision was to stay at home with my son and optimize the hours during the week and weekend working with the young guys. I was extremely committed to both jobs even while my wife and the rest of my family were still priority. My wife and I had to make a few modifications occasionally, and she continued to support all my endeavors. She deserves credit for being the brains of many of the proper decisions with networking and technical business practices. I'm the hands-on guy who highly enjoys dealing with the serious matters. Separately, I made a choice not to continue advertising with our youth agency. Although marketing was a part of the plan to expand our agency, I had to be realistic about too much growth at the wrong time. I did not want the quality of service to suffer because of unduly pursuing more business for our agency. Keeping my reputation intact required me to revisit the theme of our agency: "Investing in the lives of our youth." It was important for us to maintain quality over quantity. You control your reputation. Navigate well!

Reputation really does matter. I do not recommend alleviating marketing and advertising from any business. As a business major in college with a concentration in marketing, it was totally averse to the appropriate business practices and techniques acquired in school. How did this seemingly counterproductive decision work for me? My reputation with young people was the overwhelming factor. The tremendous amount of parents, guardians, grandparents, young men and professionals were instrumental in my ability to thrive without advertising. The advantage of word of mouth was a proven tool that profoundly affected our agency in a good way. Also, credit goes to the many young men who gave me such a challenging time initially until I earned their respect and trust.

Ms. Dee and Ms. Michelle are two professionals toward whom I express extreme gratitude. Those two women empowered me with getting the agency off the ground and believing in my ability to connect with young people. In fact, Ms. Dee referred many professionals to our services because of her confidence in my ability to effectively imbue the lives of young men. Some of those professionals who were referred to us recommended more children to receive services from our agency. When people are willing to support your vision, please remember to humble yourself in the presence of the Vision Giver. *And when he had seen the vision, we [including Luke] at once endeavored to go into Macedonia, confidently inferring that God had called us to proclaim the glad tidings (Gospel) to them (Acts 16:10).* My wife and I continued to remain steadfast in the promise of God regarding our agency. Conversely, there were a few times when I felt close to being defeated and unable to overcome obstacles with business requirements and adversities. The Lord is faithful! You may not have extreme wealth, but there are not too many things that exceed a man of his word. In addition, wealth alone will potentially make you feel isolated. Enjoy resources, be a good steward, but be aware of meaningless paths!

CHAPTER 7

***

Youth Counselor and Mentor

Gather Valuable Experiences

THERE ARE A tremendous number of youths who attributed to my success as a father. I had the privilege of working with hundreds of young men before having a biological son. These young men, as well as their families, deserve much of the credit for making me into a quasi-prepared father. In fact, many young men have frequently called me a father figure in their lives. I understood their sentiments, and it created an ambiguous feeling regarding their reasoning for expressing those thoughts. I felt capable of handling the responsibility of being trustworthy as a father figure, but I knew at some point my relationship would come to a conclusion with many of those same young men. How did I handle short-term relationships with young men?

I continued to learn and equip myself to become a better mentor and counselor. In fact, I learned a valuable life pursuit from a professor at Howard University Divinity School. He conveyed the significance of understanding the condition of people during one of his lectures. As I reflect on many young men in my ministry work, the majority of them were seeking sufficient time from a man who could provide some simple attributes; compassion, trustworthiness, understanding and hope were some of those qualities. In addition, it takes time to identify, unravel and confront the complications young men are experiencing in life. As a result, I recognize the value in listening for understanding and not to respond in an expeditious manner. Approximately 12 years later, my professor's encouragement remains a standard in my approach and perspective toward young men. It is no easy task, but I enjoy this calling of leading and influencing young men. On the other spectrum, I glean a great amount of insight from young men, which empowers me in my progress as a father.

If you are not endeavoring to gain an equivalent amount of knowledge in conjunction with teaching young men, it will potentially become very frustrating for the young man in your life. Being creative matters! I observed an ongoing pattern with many of the at-risk youths. First, most did not have a reliable man in their lives. Secondly, they were so jaded with the same talk week after week. Allow me to present the transparency expressed to me from some of these young men. They were frustrated with professionals coming to work with them for just another paycheck. Some of the young men just needed someone to listen attentively to them express their hearts. Even as leaders, we simply talk too much and listen poorly at times. It is intriguing, because many young men did not want to work with me because of the reputation of other counselors. I did not have to say anything, and some of them wanted nothing to do with me. It was not personal on their part.

In many instances, they could anticipate and predict the words before I spoke them. But there was a silver lining in the clouds. I can accurately say that the hearts of most of them became receptive to listening, and a high percentage of young men came to respect, trust and seek me over these past 13 years. Did I mention it is not always an easy journey? At times, influence is not really influence until you recognize the power of endurance during the most severe test. I must acknowledge that I had many learning errors and a tremendous number of young men were patient enough to teach me especially, as a rookie counselor. I'm really benefiting from valuable qualities displayed by these young men, and I owe them a heart of gratitude. They did not quit on me, and I learned innovative ways to replenish my heart with courage due to a countless number of great young men.

Two of my beneficial qualities and tendencies are my tenacity and determination—qualities attained in Philly. They saved me countless times during my early years as a professional counselor. It is virtually impossible to make me quit or give up. However, if you have only tenacity and determination, you may still fall short with influencing young men. They may not admit, acknowledge or comprehend their desire to receive love, hope and care from a man. However, I have noticed the importance of those qualities. If young men do not earnestly and consistently feel you care, they will reject you. Fathers especially should be mindful and careful not to leave our sons in a condition of long term meaningless living. If you have been unsuccessful as a father, do not throw in the towel.

Self-depiction as a Mentor

I have absolutely learned valuable lessons in my quest to improve as a mentor among young men. There are so many young guys that I connect with in a powerful way, and I continue to be grateful for each positive rapport with my young guys. Most of the time, I truly feel like a father figure to these young men. However, I never cross the line by putting pressure on these young men with the same responsibilities that I reserve for my own children. In my opinion, it is important to distinguish your role while simultaneously empowering parents to reach a level of heightened responsibility. I love mentoring so much that it feels like second nature to be involved with the lives of so many young men. I must first acknowledge that listening and learning from young men are two of the most important attributes for me while attempting to be effective in guiding them. Allow me to give a detailed description of my mentoring self- depiction.

QUALITY

I view myself as a mentor determined to teach values, life goals, work ethics, honesty, persistence and other qualities. It is always important for me to remain cognizant that I will never be perfect while working with youths. Therefore, I do not mind sharing appropriate imperfections in my own life to better connect with young men. God perpetually keeps one major focus for my work with young people. If my life was able to be transformed, then any young man can achieve a renewed life. Why? Simple, God can do it. There were many self-traps that I allowed to envelop me. The ability to have freedom over those strong entrapping grips empowers me to understand the liberty awaiting other young men. There are various times when I face challenges in mentoring young men, but that is just part of the process. I believe some of the greater crucibles occurred in my counseling days during the first couple of years. There were so many formidable situations with many young men, and I did not have the experience, faith or wisdom to counter their problems in a highly effective manner. Even during my early counseling years, God was developing the quality of my character for this current time with young men.

FAITH

In life, we hopefully grow and mature instead of remaining complacent with partial success. However, the game changer is God reminding me to not give up on young men. There were times it took months before I was able to make a sound connection with young men. For some reason, I really flourished while working with young men trapped in gang life, defiance, disrespect, oppositional behavior and violence. I recall one particular gang-related young man who refused to work with any other counselor except me. I always enjoy getting those calls from professionals because a young man wants me to work with him because of a prior working relationship or my reputation with youth. Nevertheless, it still does not make influencing young men any easier. It is serious work especially behind the scenes. Prayer, wisdom, courage, love and respect are some of my greatest tools. However, the proper influence means we should address our deficiencies as leaders. I certainly acknowledge the importance of becoming increasingly influential as a result of working on self-weaknesses. In addition, you have to earn a connection with young men. I'm very grateful for working with hundreds of young men, but I can say in a forthright manner that there a few young men that I did not reach at the highest level. No self-condemnation! They taught me more about myself in those difficult cases. I thank God for every transformed young man and the young men who helped me to expose some of my leadership errors.

PRINCIPLES

There were four principles that were important for me during the first couple years of counseling and mentoring. In fact, these same values continue to be a pillar in my work with young men. During my initial visit with young men and their families, I would stress the importance of trust, respect, belief and honesty regarding the mentor–mentee rapport. I also express how it is never just about the mentor teaching the mentee but the relevance of teamwork skills to ensure becoming successful in accomplishing the necessary life-enhancing goals. Mainly, the four aforementioned principles (trust, respect, belief and honesty) were more critical for me to apply in my work with young men juxtaposed to those same qualities being expected from the young men.

TRUST

Trust is such a paramount asset when leading young men. I would normally verbally express to them ways to develop trust in relationships. But nothing compares to leading as a trustworthy individual. However, there are countless ways to build on trust with young men, and it really depends on their situation. I find myself using sports, exercise, walks, books, animals and other relevant connections as a foundation. Subsequently, I attempt to reach them beyond the surface matters. It is also highly important to understand one's God-given gifts. I continue to work on developing my forte in some areas, but I'm also aware of the power of faith. In addition, I recognize the importance of networking with other appropriate resources. Trusting in the abilities of others will provide additional resources and an opportunity for young men to trust in the integrity of other competent and qualified leaders. So I view trust as an ongoing assignment, which requires the proper focus, diligence, attention, determination and action. It does not take much to dishonor trust among young men, so consider your words and actions to avoid disqualifying yourself as a noble influencer.

RESPECT

I have also learned a valuable lesson regarding respect while attempting to influence young men. They will make you earn their respect in most cases, and I will argue that it is done on a trial basis. They will evaluate you until they are able to reach a full level of trust with the influential person. It does not mean we must be perfect with young men, but as leaders we are held to a higher standard than others. In some instances, young men are watching to determine the scope of trust to give to us. Therefore, teaching young men the value of respect requires an understanding of self-respect. Without a measure of self-respect, it becomes cloudy on demonstrating it to others. If you listen closely to young men, many of them struggle with this thought of being disrespected. I also have observed young men who struggle with insecurities, and it heightens the illusion of feeling disrespected. How do we help them fight disillusionment?

I could not possibly enumerate the young men unwilling to respect any authority figure attempting to help them. It is something encountered on a frequent basis. Is it possible to respect young men when they show nothing but disrespect? Please take the time to ruminate on your answer. In order to help fight a young man's disillusionment, I attempt to identify his needs. However, it is also urgent to consider all the internal, external and pragmatic requirements to effectively work with young men. In other words, I must equip myself contingent on the young man in front of me. At times, it may require receiving additional resources. There is no shame in extra qualified assistance. Moreover, I find myself making modifications in my approaches as merited. One day I might be potent in my endeavors with young lives and the next day experience a restored individual. So I say, "There is no specific formula to teaching young men respect except my reliance on the Lord with each life entrusted to me."

Of course, I engage them in the verbalizations and practical tools for self-respect and respect for others. I'm not promoting an anti-book approach or other useful resources for teaching young men respect. But personally, the greatest asset for me continues to be an ability to come from a place of care and compassion for each young man. For some reason, it brings me good results. In a recent conversation with my wife, I discussed my desire to enhance many other areas that are shortcomings for me. I entreat you to never be afraid of telling yourself the truth. I like to say, "Self-examination is your friend." When you establish yourself as proficient in one dimension, then it is time to put energy into other depleted areas.

Belief

You want to avoid an improvident perspective in your involvement with young men. We will need to believe in seemingly improbable outcomes.

When we limit our vision of what young men are capable of becoming, then it can deflate their self-initiative. I never encourage being dishonest with our influence. But we should not relegate them to a status of impotence because we fail to move beyond our own judgmental conclusions. Your inability to be fortified in vision alleviates the hope for the person entrusted in your hands. If you do not trust in your ability to be successful with them, allow yourself to move forward with integrity and honesty. There may be other resources more suitable or a need to collaborate with additional professionals and leaders. Do not stunt their progress because you are unwilling to deal with the challenge.

Honesty

Honesty with young men continues to be an interesting dynamic. There are times when being honest with them will not translate into their being honest. You will discover that it demands strong investment and avoiding some uniform approaches or practices. In my experience with young men, they will do as much as possible not to disappoint you when you are trustworthy. It does not resolve every life issue for them, but it does give you an authority that was not previously appointed to you. I refer to honesty as an interesting dynamic, because it will take time to assist a young man with being transparent with you. Being honest is not some fairy tale approach to forcing him to become the person of your standards. Be careful of attempting to take control of his life in a demanding way. It is vitally crucial to understand each life you are dealing with despite the commonalities with other young men. There are many times when I had to deal with my insufficient skills and preparation. However, my rapport with young men enormously benefits from the values that I express to them. In fact, many of them draw closer in their relationship with me due to honesty and non-judgmental approaches. Leaders benefit from maintaining an understanding that it takes time, investment, research and other imperative endeavors for change. Are you doing your part? Therefore, let us be prepared to be honest with ourselves as influencers, so we do not present any false, misleading or unrealistic disadvantages to our young people.

Lead with Teamwork and Other Foundational Approaches

Words really matter when I'm interacting with young guys and attempting to influence them in a meaningful way. I would rather not call my young guys "clients." It really is a personal perspective, and it leads me into viewing them in a positive fashion. The chemistry necessary for influencing young men exceeds a business rapport. So there are times when I just go with the flow of what seems right and not what sounds politically correct. I'm grateful for three new approaches regarding my rapport with young men. First, I have a great affinity and connection with young men that surpasses viewing them as clients. Second, I remind young men of the need to participate as a team. I have recognized that I will never become successful with young men, if they are not committed to teamwork. So I infuse a sense of responsible behavior in them through emphasizing the need to "do your part on the team." Influence grows in its potential when those being influenced are galvanized by their personal contribution toward the ultimate goal. Finally, I use a notebook for gathering inspirational, corrective and productive concepts for each young man's life. It is sort of a memoir for the young men to treasure for the future years. It also allows me to capture some of the profound discussions in a visual manner while following the progress of each young man. Whenever you involve teamwork, then you can resuscitate some of the most valuable moments from the perspective of the mentor and mentee relationship. Never undervalue the power of influence through teamwork. In fact, become stimulated in all the great things that arise from the teamwork with your son, daughter and other influenced individuals.

Recognize Potential Early

I have seen a pattern with young men doing well and demonstrating potential during their early stages but encountering destructive lifestyles as teenagers. There are many mothers who share stories of sons being model children as young boys, but something rigorous occurs during those adolescent years.

Let us not attempt to use a blanket solution for this problematic situation. Remember, it takes time to understand the condition of each unique issue and person. Therefore, it could be irresponsible to say it only takes doing one specific action to resolve or transform lives. There is some real pain that young people are experiencing and are ill equipped to handle in many cases. What can be done?

I believe it is vital to recognize potential and then influence young people unremittingly before the ongoing trouble initiates or persists. Furthermore, we should seek potential and not just choose a culture of youth whom we deem as important investments. How do we accomplish such a task? Well, it depends on our willingness to be earnest with investing in the lives of our young people. Fathers will need to take a leading role in this journey.

I want to remind all young people who are struggling with life that you *do* have the potential to overcome. *Yet amid all these things we are more than conquerors and gain a surpassing victory through Him Who loved us (Romans 8:37).* I find it very humorous when people will exclusively support you if things are going well in your life. But you will not find them when the rough times occur. Many people have encountered selfish and agenda-oriented individuals. Being used by others does not feel good. Nevertheless, I revel in those young men who are considered underdogs and who are undervalued and thought incapable of a productive lifestyle. It motivates and compels me to guide them beyond their seemingly insurmountable circumstances.

Learn from Special Influences

I certainly forgot about some of the many influences from young people over the past 13 years. A substantial number of young people have made a difference in my short- and long-term decisions and actions. They all deserve credit for their ability to stir up transformation in my life. I really feel indebted to these young men for their inclination to imbue me through sharing their stories. There are many events that I experienced with young men that have been the impetus for elation in my life. I have not forgotten my young guys who beat the odds by graduating high school, getting that first job, attaining a driver's license, getting married, having a child, are college bound and many other accomplishments. You guys will always be like little brothers. But I want to share two influencing stories that come to mind.

Baptism and Renewal

I was glad to have the privilege of baptizing a young man that I knew for years. He (Brother Norman) gave his life to Christ, and he did not allow anything to stop him from responding to the internal influence occurring in his life. Christ does the calling, and it could happen to some person that you may not expect. I will always be grateful for this young man stepping out on faith in such a time of uncertainty, peer pressure and various life challenges.

I really know influence for my life will never be relevant without trusting Jesus for the answers to the otherwise perplexing issues regarding my responsibility to young men. Giving up on young people is not an option, because I know the One who handles options perfectly. Stop relying on your finite strength so that you will persevere when the heartaches, headaches and impossibilities attempt to overtake your thoughts concerning the underdogs of life. Make yourself available to open the eyes of young men, especially through your private prayer life. So it will require prayer but also an investment in the pragmatic work for that young man. Who will compel him if you do not take the time to invest in him? Brother Norman, I will not forget the time we spent studying God's word, praying and talking about ordinary things in life.

A Young Man Compelling Others

Another young man greatly encouraged me with his hunger to see others become set free just like him. I remember visiting this young man subsequent to prayers and doing some practical work in his life to overcome challenges. Although he did not have everything together, he was extremely enthusiastic about the liberating feeling in Jesus. During this particular visit with him, it was easy to sense the renewal and restoration going on in his life. I could almost reach out and touch his life alteration. He went to school and also got on the telephone to tell his friends to try Jesus, so they could experience true freedom. This young man cried and hugged me, because his life transformation was authentic. Incredibly, this was a young man who never became emotional, and he usually did not express any deep thoughts about God. Keep going, brother, because God is the only one that knows the heart. On the way, encourage another heart.

Compel Them Now

I believe the ripe time to influence young men is when they begin pursuing me for answers or seeking me out from other people. (Texting can be resourceful). In those instances, I will usually attempt to go out of my way to connect with them expeditiously. Take advantage! You may not get another chance. Be prepared to sacrifice. There are times when young men are experiencing perilous times in their life, and they will only share it with those individuals who they consider trustworthy. At other times, compelling them will be a matter of dropping everything you are doing just to be a listening ear. You develop a deeper rapport when you are available to converse about matters close to their hearts.

During these times, it is important for me to "remain still" and listen attentively. Nothing is off limits. So it is no surprise when young men solicit me for guidance on relationships, fear, spiritual issues, distrust, academic challenges, family problems and even a willingness to share positive events in their life. I really enjoy the good news because it replenishes me with strength. Truthfully, they are looking for you to lead them in the path of liberty. They will not tell you that is what they want from you. In many instances, they do not even understand what they need in life. But they are seeking a word that will bring them nearer to peace in their life. Why do you think they came to you in the first place? They had a plethora of other options? In particular, they could have kept to themselves.

They may not share issues with their parents, but they will share them with you. Why is that the case? We could answer that question with multiple answers. Choose your answer to this question and muse on it. Be careful not to misuse, mislead or misinterpret your authority over their lives. I want you to remember when those you influence invite you to engage in confidential dialog, it is probably because of something special that already occurred in your time with them. Do not take it for granted. You have potentially compelled them previously without noticing the depth of your influence.

Most times, my young guys are respectful toward me and careful not to use offensive language. Even when they use inappropriate language, in most cases they will attempt to recant profanity- laced sentences as a sign of respect toward me. We have all either heard or used inappropriate language at some point in our lives. So I refuse to hold their inability to communicate emotions effectively against them. But we should always challenge and charge ourselves to speak and lead young men with veracity. They are paying attention to us, and they will benefit from our courageous steps either now or in the future. I do appreciate the level of respect given to me when they are in my presence or conversing with me on the phone. Mostly, I want to lead by example so that they will not transition negative language into environments that will judge them harshly.

I'm also learning ways to influence J.D. when he yearns to receive instruction and become influenced. There are times when my son will initiate singing gospel songs and express words of praise spontaneously. So I make sure to join in with him. I also recognize his natural tendency to become influenced by his eight-year-old sister. Azaria holds so much influence over J.D.'s life that it almost seems unfair. However, I teach her the responsibility that comes with being a leader. Although J.D. tends to pick on his big sister, he looks up to her tremendously as a leader in his life. Influence passed down will require you to value, monitor, and develop your investment.

J.D. will summon me to come upstairs and do pull-ups with him on the work-out equipment in the bedroom. Azaria does the same thing. He is progressing swiftly with his exercise regimen. It is a real treat to witness during his work-out times. He also makes me laugh when he attempts one hand pull-ups. One step at a time, Son! The ability to influence requires us to take advantage of reinforcing the positive activities already instilled in our children. Follow through! Enjoy quality time! These are two factors that seem to create complications with many well-intentioned fathers and influencers. I have identified these two components (follow through, quality time) as the recipe for positive results for J.D. and Daddy. What areas do you recognize as advantages or disadvantages within your influence? Once we identify the problematic issue, it is up to us to do something about it.

I have absolutely observed the benefits of doing better as a trustworthy leader in those two categories while influencing young men and J.D. I still have significant work to accomplish with young men and my four children. But making progress enables me to be productive. In addition, you should remember that influence could be a matter of interrupting your schedule for the sake of investing in a greater prize. Your son! Your daughter! Your mentee! What next? I trust there is always room for the next thing, situation, individual, goal and mission to diligently pursue. I would encourage you influencers to also be compelled when the moment is ripe. When you compel young men, be sure to develop adequate strength to soar beyond your normal boundaries. *For I have satiated the weary soul, and I have replenished every sorrowful soul (Jeremiah 31:25).* The ability to compel others will demand from us an activated self-compelling mode. Do not forget to consider the attributes that ignite you to become self-motivated. Use all the gifts of God that strengthen your mind, body, soul and spirit.

Undertake Volunteering

I entreat all mentors to connect with their mentees in the privilege of doing something for others from the heart. There are three volunteering opportunities that I continue to involve young people with pursuing on a regular basis. My wife initiated the blanket giveaway to the homeless people several years ago in Philly. The other two volunteer opportunities are the dog kennel and equine rescue farm. In my experience, volunteering side by side with young men allows them to witness your determination and passion to help others and not only to instruct them to do all the work. It assists in developing positive teamwork, trust and good work ethics, to name some attributes.

The blanket giveaway to homeless people actually started when my wife and I lived in Delaware, and she felt compelled to give away blankets and toiletry items to the homeless people in Philly. The cold weather gave us a greater impetus to go out and demonstrate our care for those experiencing extremely difficult living conditions. We took our oldest children with us, and they fully participated in empowering the lives of other human beings. There is no greater experience in life that supersedes the ability to give to others (spiritually, emotionally, physically and materialistically). I trust Imani and Decor were humbled by this experience and will be able to pass it on one day.

I deeply appreciate young people engaging in positive activities. So it gives me great pleasure when I go to an equine rescue farm with young men who get to work with other young people. During our time at the farm, they are able to become educated about horses, develop skills, use machinery and socialize with peers without using their electronic devices. Horses are some extremely powerful animals, which have intriguing and unique personalities. In the past, I never spent any quality time around horses. But I learned relatively quickly that they are smart animals that seem to sense whether you are afraid of them. If you do not establish a rapport with them and lack trustworthiness, then it could be a challenging job working with them.

Most of all, I love the husband and wife, (Ms. Annie and Mr. Steve), team that continues to literally open their doors to invoke all young people to reach a higher plateau of accomplishment. When connecting young people with networking opportunities, it is imperative to consider the leaders in the program that will make an impact on the lives of young men. The equine rescue farm provides ample scenarios when young people are uplifted by the horses. But I also enjoy the significant connection the youths gain from a competent and caring couple (Ms. Annie and Mr. Steve) who perpetually give from a heart of humanity. Young people enjoy being in their presence, and they are enamored of people that genuinely care about their best welfare.

It is the perfect connection for young guys and these awesome animals. I will acknowledge that young men have some reticence and uneasiness about having a rapport with just anybody. You really have to earn an advantage in the relationship through consistency, trust and the ability to care from the heart. Young men and horses have something in common. They are able to distinguish the appropriate time to trust. In many cases, you do not stand a chance of getting close (figuratively speaking) to them (young men and horses) prior to a thorough examination. It is absolutely clear that young men and horses will keep their distance when they sense instability or feel uncertain about an individual. In my estimation, whenever you tame the heart of a young man through God's unconditional love, then everything else will ensue with time. But the heart of the influencer should be transformed prior to helping others with their hearts. When the influencer's heart becomes renewed, then you value the change of heart necessary for others.

It is said that a horse does not know its weight when it steps on you. I believe we do not know the weight and heaviness of hurting others through poor choices, the weight of our negativity, dishonesty, infidelity, promiscuity or a fear-induced lifestyle. It is a heavy load that many of us are carrying, and it follows us in various relationships and for the long duration. Stay mindful of negative influence being transferred to our youths because of a negligence of not understanding your power. Young people need us to know our weight of influence.

The other phenomenal establishment and volunteer privilege for youth involves a local dog kennel. It continues to provide me and the young people with the ability to socialize with professionals, engage in various work duties and learn ways to handle so many dog behaviors. I did not realize how much I did not know about dogs. Dogs are my favorite domestic animal, and it continues to be an informative and educational experience spending time at the dog kennel with the young guys. One of the greatest assets with volunteering at the dog kennel is putting young men in a position to become influenced by abilities and skills that were previously hidden in their lives. Once again, I attribute the leadership of a sound leader, Ms. Carla, who demonstrates no parameters in her untiring commitment to animals.

I always feel confident about bringing my young guys around Ms. Carla and her staff of dedicated workers. The staff usually finds the time to inform me and the young guys about assisting them at the dog kennel with various duties. However, they have sacrificed an ample amount of time teaching us important details that I frequently feel comfortable enough going to the dog kennel to volunteer without any instructions from the staff. I also attempt to lead young men to become studious in their listening, so they can take the initiative and increase their responsible actions. Being prepared to accomplish life tasks makes a difference for young men striving to become life achievers. The ability to influence at a dog kennel may appear to be uncanny, but stranger things have happened in life. I'm grateful for each person at the dog kennel investing kindness, friendliness and patience toward all of my young guys.

Compare Intelligence versus Heart

I'm contrasting intelligence and heart as an example, but it does not mean you are limited to one or the other quality. There are times when things look good on paper, and they do not equate to any substance when encountering practical matters. As a counselor, there were many times intelligent and well-credentialed individuals attempted to mainly utilize book knowledge and other failed measures to engage young people. I'm not disputing the significance of intellect or attaining college degrees. I was a college student for more years than I want to think about. However, I learned a valuable lesson about working with families and influencing young people.

In my experience, you will not last long or persevere if using only book knowledge and counseling studies when engaging most young people. I witnessed a turnover rate in the counseling field that was more fluid, capricious, turbulent and *drastic* than the fast food industry. In my assessment, some of the unsuccessful work and high turnover was due to individuals in authority not completely invested in the lives of young people, along with other reasons. More directly, there were professionals who lacked the internal fortitude necessary to overcome the personal challenges that come with working in the human service field. Your heart must be in it completely. Young people will dismiss you quickly, and they will not waste their time on rogue professionals.

In fact, professionals who authentically care will encounter some oscillating situations while working with young people. A higher level of investment in the welfare of young men will create a greater demand on your commitment. As a result, there will be adversities that need to be confronted with young people. The metaphorical "tough skin" is necessary. I have requested professionals to assign me young men with the tougher situations. One of my most prolific learning tools in the counseling field was using my ability to not take things personally. I learned ways to overcome obstacles while working with youths and remain determined to endure frustrations and impossibilities. If you hold grudges against young men, it will further distort and deter them from releasing their genuine thoughts. When you move beyond the personal dynamics, it means you value the young person above your ego, pride and other internal impediments. Otherwise, you could become another statistical example that stunts the development of a young man. Humility will be a game changer in your influential goal and destination with this valuable generation of youth. I also applaud the many leaders aspiring to influence our youth through pure love for a generation of young people. My children have been the recipient of those great leaders making a difference in their lives, too.

There are some captivating results and behaviors that I recognize with my children because of many influencers unceasingly investing their hearts into my children's successes. The influence for my children extends from church, school, the library and our community. There are times when the values from me and my wife are reinforced because of those caring individuals teaching our children life principles. So I encourage all of us to spend time developing a rapport with those kind-hearted influencers making a strong impact in the lives of our children.

My children fascinate me most of the time when I leave the house to go work with young men. They appear to understand my ardor for young people, and they accept it without any obvious resentment toward me. They usually have one question preceding my leaving the house. "Are you going to be late tonight, Daddy?" I normally respond by assuring them that Daddy will check on them if they are sleep before I arrive home. The many things that I have learned from my children continue to help me with working with young people and vice versa. It appears to me that our children and young people need our heart to be the greatest influence for them.

Repay Influence

In Philly, fishing was not a pastime that came up among my numerous friends and their family. I never picked up a fishing pole until I came to Virginia and connected with my young mentees. The value of learning from those I am leading continues to keep my mind active, receptive and fresh. In November 2014, there was an opportunity to connect with a young man from the past who is now an adult. This same young man taught me how to catch fish effectively, and as a teenager he exhibited such an aptitude to teach in a patient manner. I vividly recall that characteristic about him. So it was a no brainer when he talked about teaching me to play golf.

I have only hit golf balls at a range one time in my life, and it was not a pretty experience. In my mind, I had no inclination to ever hit golf balls again. Playing golf on a course was not even an option. The ability for individuals to influence you no matter their age is often the result of the impression they bestow on your life. Therefore, I automatically conceded to his invitation to play golf, because I knew he would teach me with fervor, good instruction and a non-judgmental approach. Being non-judgmental puts you in a position to become influential and able to achieve empowering results with others. My former mentee temporarily became a mentor for me. Roles reversed! Those who were once under your tutelage could one day give you some guidance. In my eyes, my former mentee is a decent golfer, knowledgeable and competitive about the sport. Did I mention how much I love competition? I continued to be impressed by his constant unselfishness to tutor me in golf until I could sufficiently hit the ball.

Some people just want the best to occur for others no matter the sacrifice and personal challenge. Brother Tom is that type of person. Also, you do not have to have a special talent in order to influence others. Yet you do need to have your heart involved totally. Those learning from you can discern the difference, especially when you are dealing with young men. Playing golf left me with a feeling of not wanting to leave the golf course, because I could not get enough of hitting that ball. In some ways, I do not want to get too good, because I know it will be an addictive competitive game for me. Although I would strongly appreciate the rapport with others, I already struggle with insufficient time for other important matters. So I will stick with playing when time permits. Hopefully!

Whenever a person cares in an earnest manner, you leave their presence with an enhanced character and the ability to grow in self-assurance with the most unlikely activities. Golf! Brother Tom, you have poured into my life in a profound manner, and I could never repay you for it. I was influenced to believe in my ability to play well at a game that was foreign to me. Thanks, Brother! See you on the golf course.

Become an Influential Mentor

I have heard several young men express to me that I do not judge them, and it makes a difference in their desire to trust me. It gives me an opportunity to develop a rapport and influential purpose with them because of that simple non-judgmental approach. I really find it intriguing, because those same young men allow me to give them constructive criticism and decry inappropriate behaviors without feeling disconnected from me. In mentoring young men, I constantly learn so many valuable concepts through listening effectively without holding their problems against them. I also attribute a great deal of my influencing success with young men to their sincerity, care and receptiveness of trustworthy authority figures. Teamwork matters! However, reaching them on a consistent basis requires a strong measure of determination, insight, understanding and other attributes. Despite the similarities in their problematic situations, there is no uniform solution. As a result, it is mandatory for me to ask God for wisdom in identifying and pursuing the proper path.

But they first need to know you care about them. If you are not successful with compelling young men, I encourage you to attempt addressing some potential personal poor habits or judgmental perspectives and ascertain whether you have the heart for such work. There are too many times when people are unwilling to identify their own weaknesses. I really believe it is a serious error not to consider working on our professional style, flaws, deficiencies, prejudices and work ethic.

When you are attempting to assist young men with their problems, it becomes a heavier weight for them to inject additional nonsense into their hearts. Do not become stagnate in your approach because you are satisfied by your former success as an influential mentor. Past success can be misleading, deceitful and harmful to those depending on an empowering, updated, restorative and liberating word. In other words, restrain yourself from being arrogant, complacent or too self-dignified to work harder, or in J.D.'s words "hard work-work." Influence requires an ongoing connection with the Lord for daily fresh perspectives.

The true essence of influence should constantly find its worth, perspective and attachment in the possibilities of others before it actually occurs. It is not so difficult to compel a person when he understands his self-value. Anybody can influence a person subsequent to an individual becoming successful. Can you influence a young man when nobody else believes in him? Yes, if you have a heart to endure with the individual. It also takes a trust in what God characterizes the person to evolve into and not becoming entangled in your myopic perspective of the individual. Quick question! Have you ever decided in your mind that you knew what a person would become in life, then the person becomes the total opposite of your prognostication for them? Enough said! When the Lord influences an individual, the crooked life discovers a path much smoother than anticipated. Influence is never about the assigned leader, but it commands ongoing input from the True Leader, Jesus. Keep trusting!

CHAPTER 8

—————— ✳✳✳ ——————

Philly Life (Fill-Lee Life)

Accept No Substitute

I TRULY BELIEVE growing up in Philadelphia gave me the strength, hope and aspiration to become a better human being and leader. I will never undervalue how God transformed my life during some difficult times in Southwest Philly. There were so many things that *filled* my life. As a result, you will absolutely never hear me make apologies for my forwardness, boldness and earnest position about Jesus. He is the exclusive Savior of the world who set me free from the Fill-Lee life (fill Leroy's life) *According to my earnest expectation and my hope, that in nothing I shall be ashamed, but that with all boldness, as always, so now also Christ shall be magnified in my body, whether it be by life, or by death (Philippians 1:20).*

Selfishness, disrespect, promiscuity, vindictive mentality, negativity and insecurity are several challenges that filled my life. What do you need the Lord to liberate you from regarding your life struggles? He will initiate the transformation in your life. Why wait any longer? There was a time when I was ashamed of my past errors, but God continues to rescue me from myself.

Now, I continue to endeavor influencing J.D. and numerous young men to yield to a transformed mind and heart. Why? God will do it for them too. Fill-Lee life converted to Free-Lee life (free Leroy's life). There will be times when you may question if you are totally free. I trust this is not an abnormal question for many fathers troubled about their past. Do not fret. *Therefore if any man be in Christ, he is a new creature: old things are passed away; behold, all things are become new (2 Corinthians 5:17).*

God will provide you with an assurance in the most problematic situations. He loves all of us and truly wants husbands to lead wives and children with a heart for Him. During this fatherly voyage, remind yourself not to become unduly satiated, disheartened, ill-equipped and fearful. Instead, you are encouraged right now to persevere, love, trust, forgive, stand and live in a rejuvenated manner. You are the only one who can preclude you from making life progress. Continue to rumble, wrestle and scrap for the influence over your son's life and other young men waiting for a man of courage to empower him.

Learn from a Life Crisis

As a teenager, I was stabbed severely, and the young man came extremely close to killing me. Unfortunately, it was not an eye-opening experience due to my desire to take more risk, live unfocused and yield constantly to a hardened heart. Can you imagine? God spared my life, and I totally ignored His calling to surrender to Him. During these disobedient youthful years, my purpose, love and inclination to empower youth was developing gradually. The father and son influence had already been determined for my life. Guess what? Your influence with your son is already in motion as well. No matter the personal crisis, our sons need us to assist them out of the generational mess.

Anytime we face a debilitating life stage, our thinking should transcend the obstruction—not always an easy duty. What precludes you from making progress? As men, we need to attempt to answer that question. We transfer far too many poor habits to our sons due to a lack of self- examination and doing something about our various shortcomings. The life crisis continuity upon father and son (generational) will end when you decide to change. What do you need to make happen? In order to adequately respond to the question, one should lean toward self-examination, identify weaknesses, pursue truth, evaluate, execute and unceasingly choose God's wisdom. Ask God for His divine purpose in your life, especially if you have never asked it previously.

Build on Self-discipline

Boxing is one of the most disciplined sports in the world. Unlike team sports, you depend completely on your own abilities during the rivalry between you and your opponent. However, a good boxing coach matters. No excuses are acceptable, because it comes back to the one person in the ring. You must look in the mirror and learn to understand yourself. In retrospect, self-reliance was one of the main reasons I was drawn to the sport of boxing. In my experience as a boxer, preparation and courage were two of the greatest assets for success. Influence can manifest in various ways. Interestingly and ironically, boxing taught me ways to reduce negativity, violence and disrespect toward others on the streets of Philly. How? I became extremely dedicated to learning ways to improve my boxing skills inside the ring.

My boxing days provided me with some of the best life accoutrements. As a fighter, I learned ways to become completely disciplined as a young man. During those days, my healthy eating habits, running regimen, courage, work ethic, passion and ability to think creatively increased substantially. Now I use those same qualities on a regular basis to enhance my life as a husband, father, businessman and ministry servant.

Improve Through Friends

I had many close friends growing up in Philly, and I'm grateful for all of them. During each stage, all of my friends were instrumental in influencing me to become a better man, even when I did not realize God was at work. But my closest friends during my young adult life were twin brothers, Aaron and Eric. Although they were good professional boxers, I enjoyed their loyalty, love, care and dedication to our friendship above anything else. Our friendship still delivers meaning to my life today.

Grow Through Gamesmanship

In my estimation, no other game is comparable to chess. For more than 20 years, chess constantly provoked me to think, assess, choose wisely, persevere, focus and compete intensely. My father had a familiar saying when I was a youth. "You never know what you will have to do in life, so learn as much as you can while you are young." I did not completely understand the wisdom of those words during my younger years. My father was correct regarding the importance of learning. Chess is not only a game, but it is an acronym for some fatherly attributes essential to the father and son influence.

CALM

In the game of chess, maintaining a calm demeanor is imperative when facing an opponent. There are many times when your opponent will have the advantage due to various reasons. It is difficult to relax and not display some anxiety when encountering someone more skilled at chess. The pressure can oftentimes become overwhelming when facing defeat. How do you handle pressure? Many people do not like to lose in life. I'm no exception. I love to compete, but I have trouble accepting defeat especially after working hard. But I trust even defeat is not so bad if I can learn ways to stay calm during the turbulence. What is your remedy for keeping calm as a father when things are dismantling in your presence? Of course we are all unique, but I think there are some uniform methods to working through life pressures.

I will share two important calming methods utilized in my daily dealings with J.D. Preparation and ongoing thinking have been instrumental in putting me in a good position as a father. You may use whatever methods keep you relaxed. But if we are not prepared and thinking there may be additional problems to overcome, we should remember ongoing success with our sons does not mean we stop utilizing the creative development component as fathers. Keep learning and being pragmatic. Action empowers us and assists in terminating the sluggish life of procrastination. Prepare and expect great advantages when you trust the Lord.

J.D. assisted me with my preparation at a rudimentary level. I did not realize some of the basic errors in teaching my son life lessons because of some of my reckless habits. During these elementary preparation stages, I desired to learn ways to become equipped for the repetitive behavior of a three-year-old son. For example, every day J.D. was guaranteed to challenge me because of his eating habits. He would either cry when it was time to eat breakfast, refuse to eat or behave in a melodramatic way. I know you are saying this is not an aberration for most toddlers. However, it should be abnormal for fathers to respond just like their toddlers. How did I begin preparing for the inevitable? I have a simple answer. I acknowledged that I needed to work on me—not always easy for parents.

If we are willing to prepare adequately and follow through by becoming action oriented, it can become our foundation toward maintaining our composure when we are against the ropes (like in the boxing ring). It became essential to use my preparatory skills before I even engaged J.D. regarding eating his food. The minutia of life can envelop you without warning if the basic struggles are not identified and addressed perpetually. I mention perpetually due to our willingness to become complacent when we experience success. As fathers, be careful of this false sense of security. The next test is on the way. I promise you.

J.D. was certainly formidable when I was unprepared to commit to necessary changes as a loving father. There are times when we are ill informed and need to become knowledgeable instead of struggling with the typical ineffective methods. What transformation needs to happen in your fatherly approach? I encourage you to quit procrastinating. Trust God to assist you in identifying deficiencies, motivating change and filling you with ongoing perseverance. In fact, your father and son influence is partially contingent on your willingness to rectify, prepare and implement a renewed action plan.

HOPE

There were a few times when I was able to attain victory in chess because there was still hope in my unwillingness to quit. I believe one of my greatest attributes is my aptitude to never give up despite the work in front of me. Some may call it tenacity, persistence or determination. They are all felicitous descriptions. If those qualities are infused with God's wisdom, it is a recipe for accomplishments and achievements along the way. You never know when you may need those attributes for your next opponent.

Chess opponents can become over-confident when approaching victory. Mostly, in a fun, friendly and competitive minded way. No big deal! I have a close friend (Sonny) from Philly that usually teased me prior to victory during competitive chess games. There were a few times I survived some of those apparent defeats and rallied to victory. He will probably claim amnesia regarding my victories over him. Smile, Sonny; you were the overall best player between us. But it is not over until the very end. Keep enduring! It is essential to hold onto your vision, endure and stand your ground, even when the outcome appears hopeless.

ENCOURAGEMENT

I encourage you to find out some of your greatest qualities, virtues and innate abilities then invest time enhancing them. Without a doubt, I love supporting the underdog in life. I'm attracted and attached to those who find themselves in the trenches. I can't help myself. Some people say that I trust people too much. Maybe it is true. Okay, let me just acknowledge my guilt of trusting too much. However, I do think it is critically important to use wisdom. I know some people will take advantage of others' being kind. Conversely, there are still genuinely nice people in this world without any selfish agendas. I'm grateful for family, friends and strangers helping me in many areas of my life. In addition, I know God wants me to encourage lives and not live in fear. I do not feel complete or full of humanity without uplifting others in some way, especially with private prayers. *For God hath not given us the spirit of fear; but of power, and of love, and of a sound mind (2 Timothy 1:7).*

What does encouragement mean to you? Let me first start with what it does not mean. It does not mean enabling or inhibiting those you lift up. I'm still learning ways to develop skills to ensure that I do not put a person in a worse position by doing too much. Encouragement means supporting the person you are called to assist and doing it judiciously and with prudence. Otherwise, it could be counterproductive. Although your intentions are stocked with integrity, it is unhealthy to do things in disarray, especially at the expense of others. They will possibly struggle or suffer over time. But there is a brighter side to my encouragement of others. Encouragement should leave yourself and others in a position to pursue progress and utilize tools to fight through the condition in front of them. When I encourage others, it is rewarding for me and potentially liberating for them.

When playing chess I often encourage myself especially when victory is seemingly slipping away. By the way, there are numerous times when I can be a sore loser and challenge you until I win. It is a habit. I revel in competition that is healthy and empowering. I remember when Chester (non-biological father) would beat me at checkers and I would cry because losing did not sit well with me. Did I mention J.D. struggles with losing on occasions? I wonder how those competitive juices came about in his life. Of course, I'm saying that in jest. He also loves helping, supporting and caring for others at such a young age. I'm seeing some similarities. Father and son influence will one day become father, son and grandson influence.

STOICISM

Are you strong in the face of emotions? In chess, I work at remaining strong, confident and not allowing my opponent to read my feelings. Conversely, it gives me an edge when I see fellow chess opponents squirm in their chairs or give me a nervous look subsequent to making an error. Body language tells us so much without a word being spoken. People can usually determine my feelings through reading my facial expressions. The eyes are certainly a clear giveaway to my feelings.

I'm learning to use skills of remaining strong and reading J.D.'s body language to help enhance my influence in his life. Reacting to every minor fault in his life melodramatically and responding with a negative attitude is defective and contagious. I refuse to pour those issues into his life to be extended to his children. Do I think he feels relaxed and confident with me? Absolutely! I love teaching him in a calm manner to lift his head when being corrected because I want him to still experience my love for him through my eyes. I do not exclusively display a strong side with J.D. because I want him to feel comfortable releasing his true feelings without trepidation or awkwardness. God is keeping us on track with the father and son influence.

SUCCESS

What does success mean to you? This is not a trick question, and there is not necessarily a wrong answer. Success can be found wherever you have a level of achievement. Some people may equate success with their ability to gain prestige, job titles, monetary advantages or acquiring material items. There could be some veracity to that concept of success. But I want to look at success from a different perspective. Allow me to discuss two areas of personal success and ways to not allow success to define you. I will briefly address chess and fatherhood as two examples regarding my determination for personal success.

I love the game of chess for two main reasons. Competition and thinking intensely really motivate me. I'm embarrassed about revealing this next truth, but I will share it anyway. During my aspirations to compete and learn chess over the years, I would spend up to eight hours playing chess despite being in graduate school and other responsibilities. My addiction for success in chess became salient when I played for approximately 17 hours straight on the internet. Subsequently, I quit playing for a few years because of my unmanageable addiction to the game. Even success in a positive activity should be kept in perspective.

Do not misinterpret my message. In some cases, we understand it will take an enormous amount of hours maintaining your commitment in a particular field. Therefore, hard work, determination, tenacity and perseverance are qualities to be relished. Unfortunately, my desire to become successful in chess was controlling me along with causing disarray in my priorities. After a few years of hiatus, I'm back playing chess with a competitive spirit, proper time management and fervor to learn new things about the game. In fact, patience, thinking reflectively, assessing individuals and enhancing my work ethic are some qualities personally gained through playing chess.

It is also being passed on to my children and young mentees. J.D. and Azaria learned chess and enjoyed playing at three years old. Coincidentally, Azaria gets slightly frustrated when she does not beat Daddy. It will not be long before she will acquire the skills to whoop me. Hopefully, I will not complain after being defeated by an eight-year-old daughter. The goal is to continue the cycle of teaching, engaging and enjoying positive activities with the next generation. I trust my children and future grandchildren will be grateful in the long run.

At this juncture in my life, success in fatherhood is motivating, challenging, rewarding and a tremendous learning period. All of the above describe the particular emotions experienced in becoming a successful father. Certainly, many descriptive words could be mentioned regarding the abundant circumstances encountered in fatherhood.

Fathers are not typically credited with being as relevant as mothers. Have you ever taken the time to check out most commercials regarding parents and children? Mothers are usually considered the most significant parent in the commercials that I have witnessed. I'm not here to debate that one parent is more important than the other. That would be nonsense. However, I'm looking forward to husbands continuing to seek God for our resolution on restoring the family. I hope we begin to *vividly* understand the equitable significance of husband and wife within the *sanctity* of marriage. The influence of family life will become ignited through our understanding, fulfillment and action according to God's intention for the family.

CHAPTER 9

* * *

Role Models

ROLE MODELS ARE distinguished from mentors. Role models can compel individuals from a distance without personally knowing them. Mentors directly deal with mentees on an intimate basis with a personal rapport. It is good to have both as resources to enhance family, personal, business, social and recreational relationships. I want to mention one particular role model that maintained my attention for several years as a young man.

THE CARSON IMPACT

As a young man, I wanted to meet Dr. Ben Carson, a pediatric neurosurgeon and current candidate for U.S. president, rather than many other famous men. In my opinion, he was the quintessential role model, especially for young men. He exhibited some important qualities based on his standards. Perseverance, resilience, faith, intellect, work ethics, accountability and love for humanity are valuable personal qualities within a role model. If you desire, create your personal list of valuable attributes in a role model. The following are some actions I need in a role model.

Persevere

You may not be the smartest person in the room, but perseverance can drive you to another level. I classify myself as strong in some academic areas and a work in progress in other academic pursuits. But one of my greatest assets is a passion to never stop, quit or give up until I accomplish a task or goal. Perseverance is a quality that can be very beneficial. However, if you persevere without vision, it can produce inefficiency, unproductiveness and ultimately failure. We can probably find two sides of the coin in most situations if we reflect on them long enough. In most cases, I trust that it benefits us to remain diligent in our life goals and pursuits. In fact, I encourage young people to stay determined because of the many benefits of sticking with a goal until the end. The ability to persevere may not always seem like an obvious influence, but it sets us up for a mindset to endure in the most difficult times.

Strengthen Resilience

In my opinion, being resilient does not necessarily mean you are the toughest person or handle everything without encountering fear. Are you telling me you never have any reservations, concerns or hesitation in your life? Mostly, I think resilience places us in a position to encourage others, because God has already proven He will bring us through, and you trust Him on His promises. People are attracted to your ability to avert panic despite the outlook of the situation.

Own Your Faith

Are you ashamed to express your faith? At times, I was confused on using the most effective way to express my faith. As a result, there have been many times I felt an abandoning of my faith. The Lord will show us through our preparation in various spiritual tools the necessary words and actions to enforce and deliver. Do you ever feel reticent about who God called you to be in life? It can happen to the best of us. I enjoy adhering to God's strength and alleviating the superfluous pressure.

Use a High Degree of Intellect

I'm so glad of my educational experience and attending three colleges including graduate school. I also realize that influence is not dependent on college degrees but on the ongoing gifts that the Lord provides for us. Once you graduate from college, I encourage you to consistently follow your life passion and continue being studious. More important, allow your journey through the educational years to be aligned with God's purpose. It is a recipe for prosperity. Some of the greatest achievers in life are the ones who persevere with a tenacity to reach their God-intended destination. Do not settle for your finite capabilities; the Lord has so much more for you.

Develop a Solid Work Ethic

My work ethic is an important tool for me regarding the father and son influence. Would I aspire to accomplish goals effectively without Chester pushing me to enhance my work ethics as a young man? I doubt it. As a result, illuminating the obvious skills regarding my mentees and assisting them to reach greater work ethics is a priority. I enjoy working hard and not taking non-impactful shortcuts in life. It makes a difference when we are able to remain diligent at accomplishing our goals. The influence of work ethics at a young age provides us with a foundation of possessing a positive attitude and taking action at a skill we enjoy doing.

Accept Accountability

It takes a substantial amount of integrity, self-examination and honesty to be accountable. Accountability means you are willing to point the finger at yourself before blaming others when it is warranted. I have discovered taking responsibility for my actions allows others to trust me and value my friendship. I'm still growing and developing skills in this particular quality. In my relationship with my children, I have learned to apologize to them for my flaws. Being accountable puts us in a position of not being fearful of our weaknesses, errors and vulnerabilities in life.

Love Humanity

Love for humanity does not consider culture, socioeconomic status and other distractive viewpoints. Demonstrating a love for humanity means you rise above the subjective perspective in place of an objective goal. I believe one of the best assets regarding effective role modeling empowers us to address our personal deficiencies. Our love for humanity requires a skill, which means past hurts, pain and prejudices will not obstruct the vision of caring for the people in need of our talents.

Find Good Leaders

Good leaders do not need to be famous or the most celebrated people in the world. In fact, some of the leaders in my life are ordinary men with no particular titles. The leaders in my life are selected because of watching them display integrity, honesty, humility and other useful measures. What qualities do you need to observe or experience from a good leader for your life? I must acknowledge that there was a time when I would remain introverted regarding the severe trials in my personal life. But wise counsel is an enormous outlet and guide. Let me rephrase my statement by expressing that wise godly counsel is essential for our lives.

I also appreciate tremendously the significant number of friends that are ministers, business leaders and ordinary family men. It is important to select those qualified to be leaders in your life and not just anyone giving advice off the cuff. I have witnessed and experienced faulty guidance and unhealthy life advice. Also, we may need to examine our actions instead of blaming others when friendships suffer disconnections. Be receptive to acknowledging personal flaws, because it gives you the potential to open up the pathway to sound growth and progress. The great thing is that we hopefully learn from our errors as well as the faults of others. Along the way, do not neglect forgiveness, because some people are truly not aware of their shortcomings. What qualities are important for a good leader? Consider your personal list, and pursue it from start to finish. *And Jesus prayed, Father, forgive them, for they know not what they do (Luke 23:34).*

Un-Role Models

What are un-role models? They are individuals who take on leadership roles without being equipped, suitable or prepared for the tasks ahead of them.

As a result, they sometimes misrepresent, prey upon or outright deceive others. Remember, I'm not expressing leaders that simply make mistakes or personal errors. I'm referring to role models who purposely commit fraudulent, destructive, rogue and insidious actions (un-role models). What about controlling leaders? There are controlling leaders that do not realize their potential harm on the people assigned to them. Unfortunately, some leaders can behave similar to tyrants but not necessarily understand the scope of their errors. Leaders in the home, corporate world, church and community should be aware of ineffective, possessive and unintelligent leadership. There is a difference between controlling behavior and being firm. I imagine that we all have dual types of communication within us. But we need the wisdom to use communication and leadership effectively instead of in a perilous manner, especially parents. There is absolutely a place for reproving others in all relationships when merited. The Bible is clear on its teaching about yielding to authority. But I'm referring to leaders who outright mislead lives due to ego, incompetence, authoritative abuse and other illegitimate approaches. I will say it is essential to constantly seek the Lord for our leadership direction and adjustments. When we constantly behave in a manner that is driven by self-centered motives, then our influence will become detrimental. The result of unethical leaders could result in the rebelliousness of our children, congregations, employees and other meaningful relationships. Be willing to self-evaluate!

Leroy and Devina, Wedding Day, March 25, 2006

Imani (oldest daughter), High School Graduation, June 2015

Azaria and Jordan, Easter Sunday, 2015

DeCor, Azaria, and Jordan, August 2015

Azaria and Jordan, getting ready for church

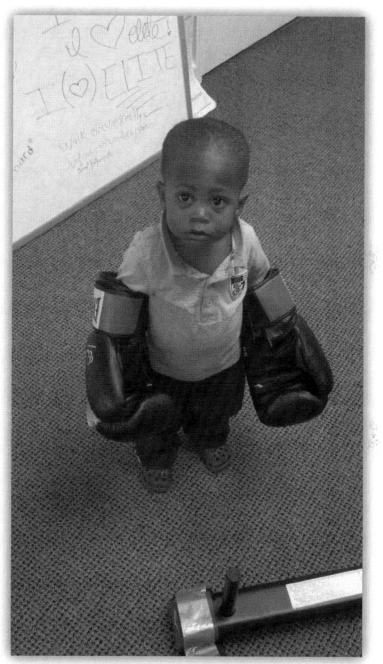

Jordan having fun with Daddy's gloves

Jordan showing off his style

Jordan catching butterflies in the backyard

Jordan riding his bike with Daddy

Azaria and Jordan playing chess with Daddy

CHAPTER 10

***

Biggest Encourager

Seek Out Reciprocal Influence

HAVE YOU EVER exercised with your son? I have learned so much regarding the influence my son holds in my life. We constantly work out together doing push-ups, hitting the heavy bag, playing at the playground and other cardiovascular fun activities. I recognize that he enjoys being my biggest encourager. As a result, I use it as motivation to maximize my workout. J.D. frequently chants my name as I do my pull-ups and push-ups ("Go, Daddy. Go, Daddy"). It usually provokes me to do additional exercise. His ability to encourage the lives of others is a powerful tool at such a young age. As fathers, we have the advantage of enhancing significant values in our sons when we spend time attempting to understand their God-given inner strengths. Have you identified any obvious inner strength in your son? I'm not a chef, but I do a reasonable amount of cooking for my wife and children. Can you guess who is right there to lend a hand? J.D. loves to season food and provide any assistance with cooking in the kitchen. Influence will roll over into other areas, especially when fathers intentionally take the time to recognize the internal gifts of their sons.

Reflect Upon Words

I encourage all people to think in a reflective manner about the talents and gifts you possessed as an adolescent. There are certain things some of us did not have to work hard at because it came so naturally to us. For example, I was always really good with spelling words, and I became intrigued with learning the definition of any word that grabbed my attention as a teenager, and it remains a positive habit in my life. I do regret taking my gift for granted and not understanding the significance of working hard to reach a higher echelon. What could we become with consistently using our gifts and putting serious effort into developing our talents?

I trust that we could become great at things that we enjoy while being natural at our quest. For some reason, I did not have to study most words, and it would still be easy to spell them in grade school. But I did not have the wisdom to consistently grow beyond the accomplishments of good scores on spelling tests and doing well in class spelling contests. When we become satisfied with small achievements, we may set ourselves up for remaining stagnate, despite the obvious potential. In my estimation, the mistreatment of potential is worse than not having it.

We benefit from self-influence of our gifts, aspirations and future goals. Again, I give credit to my mother for making me and my siblings do our homework immediately after school before being entertained by the television. It provided me with the foundational structure in my life with academics. Now, I enjoy sitting with my daughter practicing words and consistently seeing very good grades on her spelling tests and report cards. Mom, you set the path, and I'm deeply appreciative of the influence. I have also learned to *hone in* on the abilities of young mentees and teach them to pursue their talent areas.

Evaluate Habits

Take the time to evaluate your habits. By doing so, you will provide yourself with some insight on things to keep doing and things that absolutely need to be extracted from your life. We are creatures of habit, and we benefit from a sincere desire to transform the unproductive habits. Do you ever attempt changing poor habits? Many people would probably acknowledge it is no easy task to overcome habits. It requires ongoing work, thorough approaches, diligent perspectives and action.

I really believe in this next statement in a humongous way. "We would rather make other people change their habits instead of working on our personal flaws, poor habits and shortcomings." I prefer to say, shifting the blame. I especially witness this in the counseling field. In many instances, we need to influence ourselves before attempting to influence others. Unfortunately, many people are not optimizing their gifts because of a lack of seeking God for revelation on personal deficiencies.

The teacher sometimes forgets he must be open to being enlightened and informed by the student. It takes humility and other virtues to walk through some of our deeply rooted habits. It feels better to shame others instead of facing the errors of our lives. If you can relate to this behavior, then modify, monitor and measure your ways through self-examination. I trust that your ministry, career and life will be understood in an increasingly productive fashion. How do we transform the habits of others without primarily confronting our personal defective living?

J.D.'s Eating Habits

When you teach children through practice to become influenced by good habits then nothing is off limits. J.D. highly enjoys drinking nutritious drinks and participates in making them with Daddy. I have a Nutri-Bullet juicer in my home, and I use it on a regular basis. J.D. and I mix vegetables, fruit and water in the container usually with some honey (not too much) for a sweet taste, and he is accustomed to drinking for good health at such a young age. He also acquired the taste for vegetables (especially broccoli), and he will consume them in a ravenous manner. In some ways he can be a fastidious eater, but he will eat a variety of foods when prepared properly. The ability to influence with good eating habits continues to be a valuable investment for our children. Like father, like son! I strongly encourage engaging children in the details of preparation with positive activities without putting them in harm's way. Although it takes extra time to involve our sons in these activities, restrain your mindset from becoming overly annoyed with these time-consuming endeavors. Both father and son will benefit from the quality time spent in productive activities. It equips our boys with skills they will use as men. Fathers, stay disciplined. Eat as if your son's life depended on it. Influencers of healthy eating habits initiates at home.

Prepare for Opposition

Every person encounters opposition during the course of life. The way you handle it will dictate whether you will move forward or remain impotent in that situation and other circumstances. Being the owner of an agency that assists youth in developing life skills continues to bring its share of opposition. But if God truly calls us to do a work, no person can stop it from occurring.

I believe the only person that can prevent you from success with God's work is you. We get in our own way of achievement. Some reasons may include disobedience, fear, selfishness and distrust. In my experience, all of the above have inhibited me at different stages of my personal growth. We position our hearts and minds in the right direction when we are willing to acknowledge personal oppositional shortcomings. We can begin correcting those destructive vices in our life. The Lord reassures us when we are encountering adversity.

Have you ever experienced situations when you can ascertain that God worked on your behalf? There are numerous times when my business survived and then excelled because of God's promises in my life. *Peace I leave with you; My [own] peace I now give and bequeath to you (John 14:27).* The Lord consistently demonstrated His presence even when I felt inundated by the pressures of opposition, which constantly challenged my integrity. It behooves us to understand that opposition is really a disguise for your ability to attain future success, if you endure. Opposition is not going anywhere no matter how well things are presently going in your life. I discovered that embracing and enduring opposition prepares us for the long-distance battle. The influence of opposition can be an exceptional resource when paired with the proper attitude, focus, and humility throughout the process.

Allow Recreational Sports to Provide Influence

I will share my favorite basketball player and former boxing influence. In my limited down time, I enjoy watching professional basketball. If the game is not competitive, then I will instantly turn it off. It is not entertaining for me to watch a blow out in professional sports. However, there are certain players in each professional sport who cause me to be riveted to the television. I will start with the Oklahoma City (OKC) professional NBA basketball team.

The top star on the team is Kevin Durant, and he is an extraordinary talent. For those of you who follow basketball, then I'm sure many of you would agree. But I think his teammate, Russell Westbrook, is absolutely the most explosive and fiercest players in the league. His competitive nature and heart for basketball greatly impresses me. The way he plays the game appears to be a reflection of the time he puts into practicing with a strong work ethic. When professional athletes continue to remain insatiable in their work endeavors subsequent to receiving a major contract, it demonstrates their integrity for their respective sport.

Even in sports, I attempt to find ways to intertwine some characteristics and influential benefits with my approach to ministry, family and youth advocacy. When you are an ambassador for your "calling" in life, it means your responsibility and influence exponentially increases. Just remember this! Your calling should not define you, but the Caller (Jesus) always defines your true purpose. Jesus calls you to peace, love, truth and liberty. Do not abandon your priorities for Christ, especially when achieving the highest echelon of success. Stay influenced by the Influencer of your soul. *Yet I will rejoice in the Lord, I will joy in the God of my salvation (Habakkuk 3:18).*

Now, I will share the greatest influence in sports (boxing) for me when I was a teenager. The greatest sports figure for me was Mike Tyson. I wanted to emulate his work ethics as a boxer. I watched documentaries when Tyson would wake up early in the morning to run for miles and practice the art of boxing in an untiring manner. Anytime I heard the name Tyson as a youngster I wanted to glean insight from interviews, documentaries and boxing matches. In my opinion, he was the quintessence of a hard worker. I attribute a great deal of Tyson's early success to being connected with a great boxing authority (the late Cus D'amato, boxing coach). The ability to become infused with confidence from qualified leaders is crucial, especially when many others refuse to invest in your life.

When God assigns you to influence the life of a young person make sure to take time to understand the long-term purpose, plan and possibilities. You will need to envision for them what they are incapable of seeing for themselves. Mike Tyson's boxing motto was "Refuse to lose!" The attitude to never quit compelling others to transform their lives will depend on your persistence, faithfulness and hope for the impossible to occur. The ability to help young men experience something unprecedented potentially removes them from the miseries of life into a renewed life. God empowers! *I came that they may have and enjoy life, and have it in abundance (to the full, till it overflows) (John 10:10).*

Appreciate Education

As much as I love being educated from several colleges, nothing is comparable to the wisdom and power of Christ. *But to those who are called, whether Jew or Greek (Gentile), Christ [is] the Power of God and the Wisdom of God (1 Corinthians 1:24).* You will never get an argument from me about the significance of learning, reading, studying, college degrees and pursuing a higher level of education. Conversely, it was a void when I attained goals, accolades and pivotal relationships while disregarding the spiritual component of the matter. How much are you being educated, informed and empowered through your spiritual life?

The influence of using God's word outside of church makes a difference for my personal, family and other substantive relationships. What do you gain from your church influence? I did not say how many times or hours that were spent in church. I love church and being in the presence of other believers. However, if I never commit to the application of God's word, then it keeps me in a place of perpetual spiritual vacuity.

Nothing substitutes for authenticity! Becoming the best influence among my son and young men requires wisdom, truth, power and other virtues. In my personal experience, I have felt limited without surrendering to God's authority and purpose for my calling to be a leader with J.D. and the many young men in my life. When I optimize my educational, ministerial, counseling and mentoring acumen, it is due to my strength in Christ. I encourage you, brothers, to seek education in college, personally, spiritually or through some other means. There has also been a great advantage for me through spending quality time with many educated and God-fearing men. But my ability to drench myself in peace derives from exerting the power of the Lord on an ongoing basis. Nothing outweighs His sovereignty! His authority is primary in my life and makes all other influences come alive. Persevere!

Reward Yourself with Self-influence

There are several methods that I hold onto for self-influence. Some of the self-influences are truth, love, peace and self-control. My desire to influence is part of my competitive side and hunger to see great things happen. If there are no self-influences, it would be difficult for me to attempt influencing others.

J.D.'s Intriguing Influences on Me

There are various influences J.D. has on my life. I will only highlight three of those influences. First, he puts forth his best effort in his endeavors. Second, he influences me when I assist him through his errors and poor decisions. Last, it always motivates me when he questions me about whether I'm doing okay. Each influence from J.D. sheds perspective on our bond and relationship.

J.D. Gives a Great Deal of Effort

How do I know? Although his errors and poor decisions are not always fun to handle, they usually make me examine my character as well. "Are you doing okay, Daddy?" Now, this is self-explanatory. My three-year-old son wants to know whether his daddy is doing fine. It is almost like J.D. conveys to me, if things are not well with you, Daddy, then we are in this thing together (son to father influence). I always respond, "Things are well, Son," and it is during those times God is working through the influence of a son. Although it is a simple question to express to a father, his words are communicated with a serious and inward attachment to my spirit. The father and son influence at times will *inverse* to the son and father influence. I assure you that Daddy is doing okay, but I'm grateful you continue asking with a sincerity and purpose.

Recognize the True Influence of the Church

One of the errors that I made as a young Christian was relying on church as my only spiritual resource and influence. It was an absolute poor choice on my behalf. I strongly encourage you to use the influence of a relationship with Jesus, prayer, scripture study, godly relationships, worship, praise and every spiritual discipline connected to your daily living. There are too many times when people, including me, left the church premises after a great sermon never to apply the Word to our daily living. The influence of the church is only as good as the church in you. Hmmm! "That may just preach," as some ministers might say.

It can be extremely difficult in this world full of lust, temptations and depravity without being serious in your commitment to the Lord beyond Sunday. So your influence is relevant to what influences you. An individual can be inside the church every Sunday only to be influenced by everything other than the church. At this point, I hope you can at least entertain the question of what really influences your life? The current church that I attend influences me and uplifts my family similarly. More important, the ability to compel others far exceeds our duty within the church walls.

Accept Unexpected Influences

On November 17, 2014, the dental assistant at our family dentist had a conversation with me in the office. We shared some normal dialog about my family and a general discussion about our wellbeing. However, I will probably never forget what she mentioned to me on this day. I had never mentioned to anyone including my wife the desire to write *Father and Son Influence* prior to completing the book. I had approximately a quarter of the book completed, and she told me that I should write a book because of my work with young people. I just laughed at her and she said, "Do not laugh, because you never know what may happen." The real reason that I was laughing was because she corroborated that God would convey His approval of my assignment through unexpected influences.

How serious are you about influencing others? There are two young men that really made me consider the impact I had on their lives. Both young men were quiet natured and one in particular had serious trust issues when it came to men. I was humbled by the experience because of the actions of both of these young men. I was at a local store and one of these young men ran up to me and smiled while I carried my bags in my hand. He said, "Let me carry your bag," and he proceeded to discuss the progress he was making in his life. It was a powerful moment for me, because he did not have to take the time to greet me, humble himself and discuss such great news.

The next young man was especially intriguing because of our initial relationship. He was very clear that he was averse to looking up to any man in his life. When young men have been hurt then trust must be earned before there will likely be any progress in the relationship. Nevertheless, he recently expressed some positive words toward me without any provocation. More important, he took his personal time to briefly express that he just wanted to check on my wellbeing. Influence comes at some of the most enigmatic, flabbergasting and profound ways all wrapped in one. Young men will not always tell you everything initially, but if you are willing to stick with them for the long run, great things are bound to happen. Thanks for the influence, brothers, because it was an unexpected move of compassion.

Be Aware of Hidden Agendas

Not all hidden agendas should be viewed in a negative connotation. It continues to be imbuing, empowering and valuable to hear parents convey high regards for my leadership with their sons. I never want to deprive God of the credit He deserves for any successful situation in my life. Seriously! Although I work with these young men constantly, I have ascertained the only Source of my determination with the lives of young men. Thank you, Lord! When you receive extremely positive feedback about leadership qualities demonstrated with someone's child, then it feels great. However, it is a genuinely uplifting experience when parents express nice thoughts about you away from your presence, in other words, pleasurable praise expressed behind your back.

I have enormous gratitude for parents also taking their valuable time to mention kind words to me face to face regarding my work with their children. It happens on a fairly regular basis. I can honestly say there have not been any substantial negative circumstances between parents and myself while working with them as a professional. Make no mistake about it, over the past 13 years I have encountered plenty of challenges. It is part of what I signed up for as a leader among young men. In addition, we should always be ready to hear about the things we need to change. I really prefer to think in a manner that enables me to acknowledge my areas of deficiency, because I feel more focused, burden-reduced and true to myself. I have not always had the preceding mindset. So we may not always hear people verbalize their authentic feelings for us every time we meet. However, parents will find a way to share good news about you in a hasty manner because of their positive hidden agenda.

Stop Talking and Go to Work

Do you realize we actually talk too much at times without planning sufficiently for the work? How can we influence adequately without getting the job done that is assigned to us? I recognized in my own relationships and goals to reduce talking and increase action. You may or may not relate to this, but many people could benefit from just doing the job without all the extra stuff. I also realize that if I'm going to really act, then there is no need to talk about it. At times, I believe we are trying to talk ourselves into appearing genuine, but the person's heart is far from the message being conveyed. Think about it! Get busy, and that will show your real intentions. Talk cheapens the ordeal when done with unduly agendas. Remain faithful to Jesus's purpose of influence in your life. It speaks volumes without having to verbalize.

Support, Support, Support

We benefit from the ability to look beyond the errors of youth and empower young people with transforming ideals. Do not allow their personal issues to supersede the significance of the individual. I ask you the question: Have you ever been caught in some type of negative act? We are frequently too quick to focus on resolving the problem or condemn others prior to giving attention to the human being. It will take time to understand the situation, and all youth are distinct despite possible similar adverse circumstances in their lives.

I'm not implying for us to overlook malfeasance. The ability to influence means one will strive to thoroughly work beyond the life impediments of others absent of personal prejudice and condemnation. Therefore, "I got your back" means "You should first cover your back." Cover your back with what? Prayer, integrity, self-control, discipline, commitment and hope for the work in front of you. Meditate on your personal list of covering the backs of others.

Grow Through Departing Relationships

People are influenced by your behaviors, interactions and consistency. Some individuals would rather not cut ties with you. Of course, in business you want to consider the financial aspect, but it does matter when you deal with people of integrity. Do not undervalue the persuasion you carry due to the way you conduct your life. Trustworthy people can be held to a higher standard, and their words are valuable in the eyes of many people. I had a great office landlord, Mr. Richardson for several years. When he passed away, his wife, Mrs. Richardson took the lead with the business.

Several years later, I was moving forward with my agency. I enjoyed great sessions with families for years in the office, but it was time to leave the rented office space behind. It was an amazing experience to witness the landlord present me with a parting gift. She expressed her appreciation for my ability to honor my word. Your word matters! Kind words do not always come in our direction, but when they do make sure to insert them like vitamins in your system. Mrs. Richardson also discussed some positive things with my wife and put us in a better financial position because of her additional kind departing act. The ability to make an impact on a person may be ongoing without your being aware of it. It could also come at a time when you expected a departing relationship to bring about possible hard feelings. I remember during my teenage years writing the following words on paper: "Keeping your word is more valuable than having money in the bank." During my teenage years, it was a habit to keep many short writings on paper. Influence at your own risk. But it could mean an office landlord will honor you for simply following through on your word before going through a final departure.

———— * * * ————

CHAPTER 11

Use Empowering Thoughts and Words

Find the Proper Response

I FREQUENTLY EXPRESS to others that I could not stop certain poor habits without God's help. This is paramount in my life, because I recognize the Source for my ability to overcome and walk through some extremely rough spots of life. I have learned to embrace, welcome and laugh when life gives me a big punch in the gut. "God, I rely and adhere to your strength" is my hasty response to the major distractions and hardships in life. These are the times when I completely yield to God's direction, because I absolutely need His answer. It is an enormous degree of peace for my life after expressing those words during challenging times. *So then faith cometh by hearing, and hearing by the word of God (Romans 10:17).*

It relieves me from the pressures, stress, trepidation and precarious situations. Almost instantly, my mind becomes free due to allowing God to guide me through the impossibilities of life. How do you handle pressure and minimize the bad stress of life? If you are not influenced sufficiently, then your ability to adequately influence others will likely decrease.

Recognize the Influence of "Thank You"

My wife and I attempt to consistently express to our children the significance of good manners and answering others in a respectful manner. In addition, it is important for me to assist them with treating their peers with the same type of respect, not just adults. Why? The habits, love, guidance and consistency with God's word instilled in our children delivers profound results. Therefore, if we are going to hear our children convey a measure of good manners to others, then parents will need to set the standards. The influence of saying "thank you" is not just to force our children into a pattern of using kind words. But it unceasingly puts our children in a position to grow in an understanding of gratefulness. Teach them well. You decide the lessons, goals, manners and pertinent life skills. However, do not escape God's divine wisdom for ways to teach modes of sound parenting influences regarding good manners. We are not trying to coerce our children simply to respond in a robotic fashion. Teach them the meaning of the message you are attempting to equip them with in life. It does take extra time, but the investment is worthwhile.

I also enjoy teaching minor lessons to my children, such as shaking hands with your right hand. The one situation I really smile about is when J.D. struggles with looking me in my eye for too long during a handshake. I teach him to look people in the eyes when shaking hands. My son is so preoccupied with other fun things in his mind that he only desires to give a brief shake and keep it moving. It makes me genuinely laugh to observe his childish characteristics. If we look hard enough, we can discover extraordinary teachable points, even when things do not go our way regarding the children. How soon should we get started with instilling these words of thoughtfulness within our children? There can never be enough emphasis placed on the following point. "The earlier we get started with engraving, empowering and inserting virtues within our children then it sets our children up for ongoing early success." I clearly grasp the idea that many influences will not be easy to digest for many parents, because they will absolutely require you to make significant transformations in your lives. At this point, I adhere to one of my favorite sayings. "There are just some things that I will never be able to accomplish without acquiescing to God's will." *And He was saying, Abba, [which means] Father, everything is possible for You. Take away this cup from Me; yet not what I will, but what You [will] (Mark 14:36).*

I also enjoy teaching my mentees the importance of expressing good manners. In my experience, people will typically go the extra mile for you and desire to help you when you demonstrate respectful behaviors. But the deeper impact is having the mindset to express positive things even in the face of adversity. Do we teach enough good manners at home? Well, you will need to survey the interactions within your own home to give a responsible assessment on your family dynamics. I know there are many improvements, learning opportunities and growth areas for my household.

I trust that achieving the best results starts with the leaders at home. The goal is not for us to raise perfect children. I speak for me and my wife. Furthermore, we are not looking for any special attention, parenting awards and accolades. In addition, there is usually a balance to most things. If you are willing to take credit for all the good things, then you should be receptive to addressing the problematic areas. I like looking at it from that perspective, because it keeps things in their necessary position. Also, I'm grateful for the many teachers, adults, church members and neighbors who continue to express kind words about our children. By the way, I have a personality that is reasonably modest. Too much attention makes me feel uncomfortable. The funny part about the aforementioned statement is in my younger days I was ostentatious about many things. I'm extremely grateful for the transformation through God's guidance, wisdom and love upon my life.

In my work with young people and as a family man, I have taken the time to observe the correlation between the actions of parents and the conduct of children. In fact, I have noticed the parent to child interactions/responses within my own home. Although I have not completed any official research with statistics, the importance of exemplary parenting is palpable. What do you think? How relevant are your actions as a parent toward your children? Does it make a difference on how you influence children? If so, are you willing to make the essential sacrifices? Remember, we are not called to be perfect parents, but we reap what we sow, even in the realm of parenting. I strongly encourage us to become awakened to the responsibility concerning your daily influence amongst our children. Furthermore, I denounce any self-condemnation, self-pity and self-discouragement because of former parenting errors. That is not my purpose. When you have the heart to prioritize self-examination and take action, then I trust your preference to influence with purpose increases.

Seek the Better Things in Life

What does it mean to have the better things in life? The answer to this question expresses whether you will be satiated by outer things or inward growth. In addition, it is absolutely possible to have wealth and live in a godly manner concurrently. The ability to influence with wisdom and proper motives depends on what influences you. If you are acting primarily to get recognized, then this will potentially consume other facets of your life. It only means you are potentially smothered in self-centered ways above serving others. It can be transformed through developing new habits. Trust me! Truthfully, we should all evaluate, assess and understand our purpose for doing things to avert pursuing a meaningless life. For example, if you are only willing to help others contingent on some type of reward, then your influence will be displaced with selfish undertakings. Certainly, I'm not claiming to be anti-compensation. However, the better things in life should not be condition-oriented but rather what you offer without strings attached to others in their current conditions.

So I trust the better things in life are unequivocally fastened within our character and heart. What are those better things? For me, one of the better things in life is connected with holding onto a measure of peace. My stable life becomes increasingly sturdier because of the tranquility in my life. *The Lord will give strength unto his people; the Lord will bless his people with peace (Psalms 29:11).* If peace permanently left my life, then I would be stuck in a condition of emptiness. In addition, we understand that resources, jobs, education and others are important connections for our lives. But we should be aware of our primary life impetus being controlled by temporary, outward things. Therefore, my peace is inextricably linked to reliance on God's power within me. I also like when people express, "Do not allow things to control you; instead you control the things."

I remember several years ago talking to a retired medical doctor in my community who continues to help youth and other people. He mentioned to me how paramount it is to give things away. The ability to help others by giving was extremely meaningful for him. He conveyed the message, "The more you get, then it is an opportunity to give more to others." Again, he understood the importance of not being controlled by stuff. The more you are led by the Lord to give things away, the more you gain a greater abundance through depositing into the lives of others. If you have ever sincerely attempted to help others, then you probably understand the principal of giving and the gratification attached to it. More important, giving does not strictly mean how much money or material things are dispensed to others. Time, love and care are important components that leave a lasting influence.

Influence the Influencer

Have you ever felt discouraged by people not favoring your vision, intentionally or unintentionally? Never forget, people are entitled to their opinions, and if you ask their perspective, then prepare for their potential rejection. I think we naturally want people to answer favorably, because we are seeking their validation before moving forward with an idea. Although my wife and I were extremely confident about beginning our agency with young people, there were still some precarious moments. My older sister, Sabrina, was also extremely supportive and encouraging about my ability to accomplish great things with youths. In the meantime, I had to do my research and meet with other professionals experienced with starting a youth agency.

I recall a few well-seasoned professionals in the youth field questioning whether I could set up a youth agency and prosper. In my opinion, the opposition was innocuous. They simply appeared dubious about my particular style of achieving that goal. I revel in being the underdog, but I also work hard at becoming successful. Going against the tide of popular opinion will be necessary at some point in life so that you can pursue your own purpose. As a result, the *influencer* will become influenced whether he or she admits it or not. Almost six years later, we continue to make progress and inspire the lives of youth and their families. Furthermore, when you absolutely trust the Lord for making His calling on your life clear, then you have zero to fear.

Go Forward Without the Crowd

I find it very interesting and amazing when people are more consumed with the way others are doing things only to abandon their own ingenious and creative concepts. Many of us have been guilty of it, and I can speak about it from personal experience. Some people can relate to seeing something on television and saying, "I had a similar idea." However you just did not earnestly pursue it. Also, gleaning from others will always have a place in our growth and development stages. So I'm not entertaining an anti-team or anti-collaboration approach. However, it appears there are more times when people become enamored of the metaphorical new flavor of the month, because it is what everyone else is clinging too. We compromise our aptitude for success in a specific area because of our willingness to go with the crowd. By the way, I can also make the case when people go with the most popular choices in church, business, family, sports, politics and other organizations. My mother's saying still resounds in my mind today: "I do not care what everyone else did. I'm only concerned with your part." I remember those words mentioned to me as a youngster when the class was punished by the teacher for group misbehaviors. So my mother understood and communicated an important message during my early years. She was pointing out the importance of separating yourself from the crowd and showing courage to do the right thing. It is so interesting how we understand the power of our parents words after 10, 20 or 30 years. Better late than never! Smile, Mom!

There are times in the mentoring and counseling field when people are fixated on the results instead of the actual process. The results are obviously important to consider, but if we are negligent with other factors, then the results will not matter. You will potentially miss your successes without careful attention to other areas along the way. I recognized the importance of process during a business meeting several years ago. There was a professional who was so focused on going with the new flavor of the month that it appeared to impair her rationale for reaching her destination. I do understand the validity of staying afloat with all the new technology, concepts and business practices to remain competitive and relevant. However, through my experience with small businesses, there is nothing like having competent, qualified, dependable and committed people to get results. The restaurant Chick-fil-A comes to mind when I think of solid quality customer service while seemingly honoring the process of commitment to the people. In my experience of eating at their various locations, it was typically the same quality customer service.

There are many establishments that invest in quality customer service, productivity and a quality product. I enjoy supporting those businesses that value premium quality and care for the people. I'm not expecting people to jump through hoops for me, but it certainly feels awesome when the people who are serving my food do it with courtesy. The food tastes better when the people are hospitable. I know we all have our favorite places to go because of superb customer service. In addition, I think receiving favorable results correlates with developing a team of dedicated people while understanding the process. Conversely, have you ever recognized an establishment suffer in its customer service quality when the management changes? Well, I just wanted to give you something to "chew" on regarding standing out among the crowd.

Build the Position of Influence

There are times when J.D. and I are playing some type of sport in the house, and I tell him, "Get in position." One game that we play with the racquet and birdie ball requires us to constantly shift our feet. You may be athletic, confident and in good shape, but if you are not in position to be effective, then those qualities are not as outstanding. In fact, being in the right position can apply to all sports-oriented games, major occurrences and daily life circumstances. What are you in position to do? I trust that it is vitally important to prepare, practice, exercise, study and use all important measures to become successful. However, being in the right position gives you an even greater opportunity to enhance your personal attributes. If we are not mindful of our positional influence, then we will potentially undervalue, oversimplify or disconnect with the other important factors.

Let us also be cognizant of putting ourselves in a position of compromise, envy, anger, lust and outright defiance. I want us to really consider the position we place ourselves in on a routine basis. Are you inundated with life pressure because you are not able to maintain your false standards? There are various times when we are struggling in specific situations due to being out of your "called" position through God. You were not meant to go through life constantly worried, depressed or sickened by being ill-positioned. Therefore, take serious the areas in life that are enjoyable, productive, prosperous, enriching, and designed to keep you at peace through the positioning of God's sovereign influence over your life. Afterward, make sure to assist others in their need to experience life with a renewed position.

CHAPTER 12

* * *

Increased Family Commitment

I WAS ALARMED to hear statistics regarding the family dynamics regarding divorce and children born out of wedlock. During a panel discussion at Regent University, we discussed the implications of the black family. As a panelist, I remember thinking about some destructive forces among families. There is a tremendous void within the family life that especially harms our women and children. Absent husbands! Not just fathers! There is a stark difference. Before pointing the finger at other men, I choose to acknowledge my flagrant decision of not being a responsible young man many years ago. As a result, I'm included in the statistic regarding my eldest daughter, Imani, being born out of wedlock. Now she is nearly 18 years old, and I can never regain many special moments lost. There are too many African-American fathers with a similar story in their lives. In fact, there are a great number of fathers from all cultures that relate to my story. The ability to transform these dishonorable statistics must start with the man.

I will not debate the specific problems of fatherly defects and dysfunctions. They are too numerous to cover, and each situation is distinct. Some fathers are ill-equipped because they were never raised by their biological fathers. Other men (who became fathers) were influenced by unscrupulous men during their youthful years. We can point to trust issues, molestation, disrespect, resentful mothers…and the list continues. If you desire, ponder on your understanding of the brokenness within families. But allow me to navigate us through one major point, which is helpful in my ongoing endeavors with family commitment. *Preparation* is essential in my dealings for family success. By the way, this particular personal success goal benefits my marriage and family life. It is only part of the puzzle for pulling things together in my home and other relationships. It requires so much heart, wisdom, forgiveness, discernment, trials and triumphs when in the trenches of married family life. Do you agree?

Prepare

The idea of preparing is usually intended for a particular purpose and plan to be executed in the future. I truly believe some of us men have done a disservice to our sons, brothers, cousins and friends regarding preparation as family men—not all men, but I must count myself in the category of poor leadership in my younger years. For the record, it does not have to remain so dismal for our families. I salute all of the phenomenal husbands and fathers who are ambassadors for God-inspired family life. In my estimation, the next generation of sons will either suffer or prosper in family life, contingent on the efforts and action of this generation of men.

During the panel discussion at Regent University an individual mentioned that more than 70% of African-American children are born out of wedlock. The married family life (husband and wife) is suffering overtly. Pick your reasons for this marriage and family debilitation. You might even have your own remedy to this epidemic. It starts with you, so I implore you, men, to get busy with promoting the beauty of husband, wife and children through your good modeling family lifestyle. Our families are depending on us.

How do we expect our sons to become committed husbands if we are not preparing them with earnest teaching toward becoming dedicated husbands and fathers? I want to emphasize the significance of a husband being married to his wife and then becoming a father as the proper order. If husbands are going to properly influence family life, I believe it is useful to give it some necessary attention, especially while training our sons. Men, take the time to address the following question: Have you invested quality time teaching your son to wait until marriage before having sex? Usually men want their daughters to wait until marriage before having sex and neglect spending intimate time educating boys on this topic. Why?

The obvious answer to me refers to the father and daughter relationship. I have a more delicate way of handling things with girls compared to boys. I imagine most men relate to that position. However, I thank God for a wife who can address some of the deeper matters when it comes to preparing girls for life circumstances. I also take into consideration the father's perspective regarding his relationship with his son compared to a daughter. There are many ways to approach this serious subject. But I realize the need for equality involving ways to prepare our sons to remain committed to the value of God's intention for intimacy between men and women. He desires us to reserve that special moment for marriage. No debate about that truth. I spoke at a youth conference several years ago with an evangelist friend, Sister Ursula in Manassas, VA. She and her husband (Pastor Ivan) are special friends to our family and she demonstrates a deep love and passion for young people. During the conference, some of the young people had considered only the ramifications of the physical impurities and obstacles incorporated with premarital sex. If we only look at the physical outcomes, such as pregnancy and disease, then so much is being undervalued. Speaking with young people, I ask them to consider other detrimental factors to premarital sex, such as giving their heart to a person who does not care about them, feeling rejected, dealing with the pain of hurting others and many subtle traps of surrendering to sexual immorality. No self-condemnation! Earnestly trust God for the influence that prepares you for true intimacy regarding God's plan for your life.

Some may even ask are there any benefits to engaging in premarital sex. There is nothing wrong with the question. Are you ready for the answer? There is absolutely no advantageous experience of engaging in premarital sex. I have already mentioned there are some things you want to trust because of the experiences of others. This is one of them. You do not have to experience certain errors, because people have already proven the tragic outcome. People tend to mention the physical setbacks of premarital sex, such as becoming pregnant and contacting some sexually transmitted disease. But there are so many additional harmful factors.

I'm not blaming anyone else for my promiscuous lifestyle as a young man, but I truly believe it makes a difference when men tell young men about the emotional, psychological and other highly distressful circumstances that arise from premature sexual involvement. In fact, it took a love for God and self for me to transform my immoral ways into standards of respect and non-sexual activity with females starting in my mid-twenties. I was grateful when my oldest daughter, Imani, reminded me about a conversation I had with her about avoiding tempting situations with young men. In addition, my objective with all my children and mentees is to help them guard their hearts. Giving away the heart prior to God's intention will create ramifications that are not easily overcome. However, with the love of the Lord, we should continue to make progress without being tormented by our former salacious lifestyle. As you love God, then I have confidence you will find a way to love yourself. So I enjoy without any hesitation telling young men to respect and enjoy the privilege of experiencing plutonic friendships with females. *Lust not after her beauty in thine heart; neither let her take thee with her eyelids (Proverbs 6:25).*

Influence Side by Side

My wife mentioned to me recently that J.D. kisses me on the forehead good-night when I'm sleep before him. I would never know because I'm an extremely hard person to wake up and plus I snore, according to my wife. Of course, I know that is too much information. But his loyalty and desire to constantly stand side by side with Daddy continues to motivate me. By the way, my daughter, Imani, was the same way. She was always next to her daddy as a little girl. Both J.D. and Imani would cry if I left the house prematurely. I found myself sneaking out of the house many times to avert any crying from my children. In addition, I would then have to stay for an additional duration if I did not creep out. J.D. took it to another level. I trust there are many fathers that can relate to having to find an easy exit from the house to avoid causing their children any discomfort.

J.D. wants to be my shadow, whether I'm in the bathroom, cooking, reading, watching television or hugging my wife. I usually do not prohibit him from spending quality time with Daddy, but it is also important to teach him boundaries. On most nights, I arrive home relatively late, and J.D. will find a way to stay up late waiting for me. I know there are fathers who can relate to these situations. It never gets dull for me to come home to a son who only wants to chill out with his dad. I promise you that I would not trade it, despite the jaded feeling after working hard. There are times when I fall asleep and J.D. will put his arm around my neck purposely while he goes to sleep. I designate our relationship as side by side during the day and night.

The Perfect Morning Influence with J.D.

The best start to my day with J.D. constantly involves our time with God. There are not many times that I admit experiencing my very best, but in this case it applies fully. I think many people use the words "doing my best" in a very loose manner. Are people really doing their best as much as they communicate it? I doubt it, in many cases. There are several reasons that I put emphasis on the misuse of that expression. First, I think it causes us to limit ourselves from reaching greater levels in life. Second, by misspeaking any unrealistic words into our lives, it potentially diminishes the capacity to actually live them when they actually become true. Last, I really trust that experiencing our best requires us to maintain an agreement with the plans, destiny and truth of God. So I speak for myself in saying that there are certain times that I do my best, and it feels great when it happens with my three-year-old son.

J.D. finds great pleasure in the spiritual start to the day just as much as me. However, there are times when I allow him to start his day by watching cartoons subsequent to prayer. I really do not mind those days, because it is just a matter of monitoring his intake of television. Mostly, he really goes with Daddy's leadership and concedes with the plans that I have formed for us throughout the day. I enjoy when I'm focused enough to pray with J.D. in the morning to set the foundation for our day. It makes a significant difference in the way that I approach the day. J.D. and Daddy are in position to consider the needs of family, friends, neighbors and strangers. "Son, prayer time with you energizes, propels and excites me internally. Thanks for the requited influence."

It almost brings me to tears when I observe J.D. initiate his own spiritual flow, connection and worship of the Lord in a spontaneous three-year-old fashion. In other words, he does not wait for anyone to prompt him prior to giving

God glory. Neither one of us can really sing well. However, it feels good just starting the day with J.D. and the Lord one more time. J.D. typically covers our entire household in prayer even though it is just us two home at the time. In most situations, I enjoy setting the spiritual climate for our day through prayer, but there are other times when it initiates with his praise and worship. The atmosphere for prayer is set and there are no limitations, time constraints or decibel regulations for our worship of God. J.D. and Daddy have this funny thing that we do to ensure that we are not ashamed to praise God with all our hearts, minds and voices. I remember saying to him one day that I could not hear him while he was praising God. On that day, I got something started in him.

J.D. returned the favor when I was praising and worshipping God. He expressed the following in his joking fashion. "Daddy, I can't hear you; say it louder." He usually makes me smile when he provokes an urgency to get louder with my worship and praise. I reiterate to him, "Thank you Jesus. Glory to God!" We go back and forth with honoring God and encourage each other to express our love for God with confidence. It is so intriguing to observe J.D become engrossed with loving God in a fun three-year-old state of mind. This fun time together can last for several minutes while we are enjoying various ways to glorify the Lord. At times, it can get loud in my home when we really compel one another to get things going. On many occasions, J.D. is the instigator of making us get loud with our communication with God. Thanks, Son! There are no adequate words to express my experience of J.D. being by my side developing a tighter bond together with the Lord at the helm.

Reading the Bible together and watching J.D. imitate me while sitting adjacent to me is such a rapport building time. I experience the deeper solidarity between us during those moments. He will grab a Bible or another book and pretend to read just like Daddy. I peek at him and notice his serious attention to the book as if he is really reading on his own. There are even times when J.D. will tell me about things he is reading (his style) from the Bible. He will express things, such as the following. "Daddy, this says God loves us." Engaging in activities, such as reading the Bible with J.D. by my side, continues to help us build a stronger bond. We also spend quality time reading other books and enjoying various spontaneous activities. I wonder if he will remember these moments when he grows older. Will he recall the basketball games, race car crashes or exercise regimen that we engage in on a regular basis? I'm not sure.

Nevertheless, the value continues to be wrapped in just having J.D. by my side and the Lord granting us another perfect morning. The perfection is not because of me or J.D., but God's ability to spread His love over the father and son influence. Spending an enormous amount of time with J.D. daily means I must spend time with my Father God for guidance on the next influence with him. I encourage us to not skip our time with the Master. What do you experience in your perfect mornings with your son? Of course, you can have a perfect experience with him anytime of the day. Are you playing a game with him, or is it during prayer time? Remember, the influential early years of training give us a slight glimpse of our sons' potential. Train diligently! There are some things you would not substitute regarding time spent with your son. The ability to have a perfect morning with your son means during that particular time, even the mistakes make you grow closer to him.

One of the great things about influence is to know that personal shortcomings are not an excuse to quit persevering. How many times have you heard this one? "We all have something that we are ashamed of in life. But it should not preclude us from moving forward." There are times when I'm disciplined in my spiritual approach but I also realize the deeper level awaiting my spiritual life. I will probably always remember a pivotal talk in the office of a professor from Howard University many years ago. He told me, "Never lose perspective on your humanity." In other words, we are all human beings. Therefore, we have frailties, weaknesses and shortcomings that are part of our nature. As a result, we should be careful not to self-destruct. Truthfully, we frequently make things worse than they need to be in life. Well, I know that has been the case for me. Recognize your limits as well as your God-given talents. The same professor probably had a good feel for my serious natured side, and he gave me insight that continues to stick with me. So I encourage those who make their lives into a daily stressful ball of disaster that it is time to stop skipping over life's abundance. Now!

Code Words

I express certain endearing words to my wife and children.

Wife and husband code words: "Are we dancing tonight?" This is our code words for spending quality time together attempting to escape any interruptions from our children. (Sorry if that is too much information) Side note: I lack any real dance moves.

Children code words: "Give me a nip." This is how I request a kiss from my children.

Hey Bippy: I'm sort of similar to George Foreman. He named all of his sons with the first name George. I did not go that far with officially giving my daughters the same first name. But I call both of them by the pet name "Bippy."

Special times and words increase my ability to communicate in a loose and fun way with my family. Although I'm very serious natured, it is extremely important for me to balance my demeanor with genuinely showing my sense of humor as much as possible toward my family. There are numerous times when I listen to a commercial with music and spontaneously begin dancing. My wife and children always tell me to sit down and immediately shout, "Here we go again!" when I entertain them with my stylish dancing. My wife continues to point out the stiffness in my dancing style. I think they are jealous. Just kidding! I will have to learn how to stay in my lane. Unfortunately, dancing will never become my specialty.

Instant Results versus Influential Results

There are many parents who want instant results when it comes to correcting the delinquent or negligent behaviors of their children. I frequently remind myself that many behaviors took significant time to become out of control. There are too many times when we allowed things to remain untouched with our children only to witness the issue blossom into something worse. Influence is for the long duration. We will need to become cognizant of the things we inject into our children.

In many cases, it took years for them to get to their current position. Influence is not just a matter for a particular situation, person or challenge.

Influence carries with it a sense of ongoing application that becomes second nature for the carrier. Influence loses its power when it becomes diluted by haphazardly attempting to make it fit into any situation. I have recognized a greater success rate with young men through assisting them with purpose, direction, truth and a never- give-up attitude.

In my experience, pursuing instant results constantly leaves the influencer in a worse position than the one needing the assistance. He or she will become engrossed in taking short cuts and become satisfied with meager results. I would rather work with compassion, honesty, integrity and sincerity with a few instead of ill-equipping an entire group because of a lack of diligence. Be honest! Self-examine! I like to say that I do not want to make my job tougher than it needs to be with young men. Chester would tell me as a young boy, "Do it right the first time, and you will not have to do it again."

Many parents are frustrated because of dealing with issues pertaining to young men making poor choices for a long duration. They are anxious to see professionals turn things around for their household. Clearly, parents want to experience positive results for their sons. They want to see a transformation, but change requires the entire household to modify behaviors in many circumstances. I do understand young men have some obstacles to confront, but we should not neglect the greater picture. The family work! What do I suggest when things are not working out for the family? Well, it depends on the problems interfused throughout the family dynamics. But if it is appropriate, then I will suggest identifying personal shortcomings, make necessary adjustments and delve into essential, relevant action. I think one of the greatest influences as parents is our ability to become completely honest with ourselves behind closed doors. If you allow Jesus the Master to perpetually guide you through your flaws, then you could learn ways to distance yourself from feeling inadequate. Walk by faith, and bathe yourself in it. There is no greater counselor than the Counselor Himself.

My heart especially goes out to the many single mothers struggling to raise young men. I have seen a pattern of misbehaviors from young men because a single mother was not able to control her teenage son along with additional contributing factors. The influence of a mother toward a son is certainly possible. I would never attempt to devalue the plethora of great single mothers who have endured the battle in order to raise great sons. But the influence of husband and wife invested for a lifetime in marriage always brings hope to the wholeness of the family outlook. When attempting to understand the significance of family influence, I have benefited from wise counsel and ongoing study of God's word. Never give up! Commit!

In addition, I have witnessed some great single fathers demonstrating responsible behaviors and being leaders in the home. I love seeing good fathers. They are so inspiring to my life. Unfortunately, the most difficult patterns that I have observed are young men not having a relationship with any positive male role model on a consistent basis. I did not say a complete absence of fathers in each situation. But the inconsistency between fathers and sons appear to create a consistent missing element for the long term in the lives of our sons.

CHAPTER 13

* * *

Personal Growth

Influence with Variety

MY DAUGHTER, AZARIA, enlightened me through her particular style of learning to practice influence with an open mind and variety. We were playing chess one day, and she did not want to play anymore, because she did not want to lose. She abhors losing, and I usually check for tears in her eyes as an indicator to lighten up while playing chess against her. For an eight year old, she does quite well with playing chess. Most times, she does not want me to take it too easy on her. As a result, I attempt to motivate her and sharpen her skills through increased teaching and not simply allow her to defeat me. However, my competitive nature is over the top at times. One day, she is going to have to check to see if I have tears in my eyes as she continues to get better at chess. No question, she will be capable of defeating me on her own before she turns 10 at this rate. Consistency! I find making modifications to my teaching style delivers increasingly effective results.

On this particular day, I was able to enhance my ability to teach her a valuable lesson while influencing her to trust Daddy. I learned a new way to compete with her at chess and empower Azaria to build her confidence by thinking in a relaxed manner. Influence requires individuals to rely on skill, but more important, it also taught me an incredibly high level of sensitivity toward others. On that day, I came to realize the faltering thoughts I gathered about influence. In many cases, I do not always have the aptitude to make changes. There are too many times when I become comfortable with routine, even during teaching moments. But influence does not mean a person has all the proper answers and solutions. It really is not about the influencer as much as learning about the one who needs to be influenced. Therefore, influence can be accomplished in a variety of ways when you are willing to pay attention.

One of the ways my children taught me to influence required self-reflection. Self-reflection puts me in a position to correct my errors and accomplish the goals at hand. Some of my focus areas with my children are to guide, teach and live an exemplary life. I do not think it is fair to require children to uphold standards that parents are unwilling to demonstrate. So if you are showing them ways to behave in a deceitful manner, then the parent needs to make the adjustment. Some other negative parental influences include disrespect, hate, promiscuity, insecurity, negligence, abuse and harmful attitudes. Do not get caught up with the list, because all parents are guilty of something, including me. However, your influence could lose its potential value if given with the wrong attitude, motive or lifestyle. It does not mean our children should not be reprimanded when warranted. I really think authentic influence starts with the parent or guardian. Ultimately, we still have some hard work-work (J.D.'s words) to achieve parental goals.

Another way that I have been able to influence comes from witnessing the results of investing time now. I read a sign at a local juvenile detention center that expressed a saying about spending time with your children now, so we (detention center) do not have to later. The sign speaks powerfully regarding the imperative work necessary between parents and children. Just a quick note! I do not believe every child is incarcerated due to a lack of spending time with parents. In my opinion, the sign is referring to quality time, mean-ingful time and productive time with our children. I really get rejuvenated after experiencing children achieve goals because of the investment of a parent toward his or her child. Allow me to underscore the necessity for parents to recognize the power of investing time now and trusting God for the wisdom of father—son influence and any other sort of influence.

Let me take the time to ask a question. How do you handle your children when they are not doing what you said after telling them more than two times? I truly believe it could be an error to remain fixated on one particular style of influencing them, even if you are successful the majority of the time. Eventually, you will encounter a challenge that demands a different approach.

If you are not prepared to make adjustments, then the problem with your child could become more complicated. Be flexible and effective!

Use Your Abilities

I wonder if you are similar to me in this category. There have been various times when I have been good at something, yet I did not use it effectively or consistently. I trust that having an aptitude to do anything in life brings about a certain level of responsibility. Well, let me acknowledge that I have been irresponsible too many times. The great thing is I'm rectifying that particular flaw in my life. I have a long way to go, but I'm making strides toward success.

My non-biological father's words still resonate in my mind. "You never know what you are going to have to do in life." Daddy, your words still have meaning for me. I implore us to use our gifts with determination. If you are advanced at technology, teaching, athletics, cooking, nursing or any other career, then it is time to use it for good. By doing so, you are in a position to establish self-fulfillment and make a significant impact in the lives of those in need. Stay on course, and do not abandon your pathway to successful opportunities. Use your gift with purpose, love, encouragement and especially with God's wisdom.

Listen for Understanding

For a very long time, I did not consider the significance of listening for understanding compared to listening to give a response. What does it really mean to listen for understanding? It means we are prepared to understand how others view a particular matter. Listening for understanding enables us to invest in the perspective of others without prematurely engaging in our personal desire to invoke our ideas. It does not require us to compromise our values. In fact, listening intently gives me more motivation to think reflectively and lean on God for some additional help.

There are major contrasts between the two listening tendencies. The ability to listen for understanding enables you to become extremely effective at confronting the matters at hand and influencing with the proper perspective. However, listening just to respond delivers frail, shallow and an uninformed approach, especially in marriage. There are times when people listen only to respond, because they are not genuinely interested in the insight or perspective of others. Conversely, one of the ways I attempt to listen for understanding is avoiding my tendency to give my point over the valuable point of others. In a subtle manner, I will cover my mouth to suppress talking too quickly. Even when it comes to my children, I teach them this very important skill. Not only will it assist them in understanding thoroughly, but it also teaches them ways to respect the views of others.

Ask Pertinent Questions

Questions are good. Real good! I enforce an unwritten rule in my home for my children to ask questions. I really encourage them to ask questions and to discuss anything on their mind. Why? The communication that derives from their active minds sets them up for intellectual elevation. For various reasons, it seems meaningful for children to express their thoughts without feeling constrained. The influence of relevant questions enhances the insight of the one asking as well as those who were hesitant with mentioning a similar question. Can you relate to that experience? I remember being commended for asking questions in various settings, which then became meaningful for others. In my estimation, asking questions is essential for personal enhancement, knowledge, empowering self-confidence and simply getting the right answer.

Influence by Non-retaliatory Means

The ability to not retaliate when someone may "deserve" it requires discipline. There are times when I use scripture to help me in this area. I think it is vital to understand your areas of weakness and deficiency. When you understand those weaknesses, then you can choose to attach God's solution for the problem. If He did not provide His wisdom for a way of escape then I would still be stuck today. I strongly encourage you to stop waiting around for the worse thing to occur and get away before it is too late. It is a resolution that I express to many of the young men that I mentor in life. We are simply just not strong enough to handle certain temptations. Therefore, the Lord empowers us to flee before we retaliate, stumble or become engrossed in a potential harmful life altering situation. I'm speaking from personal experience.

There are times when you desire to get away from danger, but you engage in one extra word and find yourself in a heated argument or worse. You waited too long and did not reign in yourself to heed the internal warning. The Lord equipped me with the clear instruction of getting away from nonsense. Now, it is always up to me to respond in a felicitous fashion. What do you choose to do? If you were a vindictive individual in the past, then you still have the potential to retaliate despite your success in other situations. In short, know your limitations. We all have them. The ability to influence is attached to your awareness of personal defects.

The influence of the Holy Ghost will not always knock you over the head in order to make you yield to His inner voice. However, it will give you a chance to make an immediate decision to elude the incoming self-damage. The willingness to become retaliatory or non-retaliatory depends primarily on what controls your thoughts in the heat of the battle. I recommend getting away before it ever arrives to a point of great dissension. We can always deal with it another day. The most profound influence will not necessarily work if your adversary avoids truth, lives in deception and partners with unfairness. Even the most influential individuals will understand when it is time to move on because of the adversarial nature being encountered from a self-willed individual.

Abdicate Ego

As influencers, there are things that we will need to give up, which are subtle, powerful influences in our lives. Some of us are tangled in selfishness, bitterness and destructive habits. Do not become ruled by things that are non-factors. All of those things affect your ability to influence with a clear conscious. I continue to discover that ridding my life of these impediments empowers productive self-influence. The right self-influence is critical. You will forward to your children, mentees, congregation and employees many of the qualities within you. So if you are inflated with non-meaningful material, then you probably are transferring it to those under your tutelage. Conversely, you are also able to infect that same group of people with messages of hope, forgiveness, productivity and transformation. It will be up to them to apply it to their lives. You have done your job as an influencer by abdicating pride, ego and self-aggrandizement. The ability to have transcendent vision, humility, love, and discernment are some of the attributes that enable us to dissect the mass of imperfections within our characters, personalities and mindsets.

Consider Entrepreneurship

I vividly remember my non-biological father instructing me as a young entrepreneur. I use "non-biological" father instead of "stepfather," because Chester was an extraordinary influence and leader in my life. I could never relegate him to "stepfather" because of his impact on my life. (For those who use stepfather to describe their father–son relationship, it is certainly nothing wrong with that choice of description.) In addition, Chester was a prudent man. He had an aptitude for making complicated things seem simple. He made it clear to me at a young age that I should not limit my potential. So he encouraged me to learn as much as possible. More important, he constantly showed me ways to do things in a pragmatic fashion.

For several years, I was committed to earning money through cutting grass in my Philly neighborhood, starting at approximately 12 years old. It was a reasonably lucrative business for a pre-teenager. Chester taught me the basics for cutting grass the proper way. I vividly remember him making those lines in the grass with the lawn mower as he taught me the rudimentary lessons of lawn mowing 101. The rest is history, because I would save a few hundred dollars throughout the summer and purchase personal items. Even to this day, I enjoy cutting grass because of the memory of the care Chester took in my life. Do not undervalue the influence you have especially pertaining to the small things. As a young man, I also enjoyed being an owner of a water-ice business in Philly. I never stopped working as an entrepreneur and business-oriented person up to that point in my life. Chester initiated and followed through on supporting all my endeavors and always passed on his wisdom. My mother (Chris aka lady love) was just as instrumental in leading me to success. She assisted me with not settling for less and exhibited the essence of a tenacious, courageous and loving mother.

Work Hard as a Teammate

I typically remind the young guys that I can be successful with them only if they put in the work. In the past, I would work harder than some of my young mentees to deliver success in their lives. It was crucially important for me to revise some of my mentoring practices. The ability to assist young men with doing their part as teammates involves various qualities, techniques and responsibilities from the influential individual. I noticed the quality of my work improve with young men when I considered ways to transform short-comings in my individual work with them. I had to make adjustments immediately in order to rectify my lack of adequate work. Currently, I continue to enhance in listening attentively, commitment, research, punctuality, thinking reflectively, prayer, creativity and determination. When you influence through exemplary methods, then your impact will come across in a more meaningful way. There are some qualities that we should elevate perpetually with our influencing capabilities. However, we should also accept the truth regarding our non-impactful tools in spite of the depth of our knowledge, wisdom or skills. Rid yourself of toxic attributes.

There are a copious number of harmful "teammates" that I must attempt to avert. It is important for me to confront detrimental teammates such as ego, pride, selfishness, dishonesty, discouragement, unfaithfulness, impatience and hopelessness. The list extends beyond these descriptive words, but I hope you get the point regarding the need to address self-impediments. Several months ago I began assigning team names for each young mentee that described his need and our essential goals to achieve. My emphasis is for us to just believe in accomplishing the tasks in front of us. Believe! Do not leave all of the trusting to the one you are influencing; it is vital for you to believe with him. Believe what? The impossible! *But Jesus, on hearing this, answered him, Do not be seized with alarm or struck with fear; simply believe [in Me as able to do this], and she shall be made well (Luke 8:50).* Some people think the impossible only refers to the individual dealing with hardships. However, I can never move forward as an influential person without surrendering to the fact that I'm nothing without the Lord's wisdom. In my leadership role, small things can become impossible when I approach them with arrogance, non-preparation or too much self-reliance. The following are a few of the teams assembled during the mentor and mentee influence.

Show Team Determination

Many of the young men that I mentor exhibit determination. The question for me becomes how do I assist them with fostering their determination in the proper place consistently? I mainly attempt to lead them with care, trust-worthiness, hope and necessary encouragement according to each young guy. There are various times when I do not witness young men making immediate positive choices to enhance their lives. It really helps me not to judge them when I feel like they could do better in life. Oftentimes, I remind myself that it is not a personal attack against me. Many of the young men that exude self-determination are battling so many other forces working against them.

In many circumstances, they have become resigned with simply making it through the day without any significant life progress. However, I absolutely recognize that there are frequently times when they are at a disadvantage. As parents, leaders, mentors and authority figures, consider the various messages being inserted into young people directly related to your guidance. If your lifestyle, words and actions are toxic toward young people, then the responsibility is yours to make the immediate adjustments. Are you willing to change for the sake of your child? I go back to an important and necessary theme for my life. There are some things in life that I will never be able to transform without depending on the Lord's truth. We should be careful of the habits that we assist our children with developing that rip away at the core of their determination.

Conversely, I'm always grateful to experience a significant number of young men who seek me for guidance years later. It happens more than I would have imagined. Furthermore, it occurs with young men whom I would least expect to return for an injection of determination. Unfortunately, one of the greatest impediments for me continues to be a lack of sufficient time to connect with all the young guys on a regular basis. Not enough time! But they are always appreciative of my aspirations to stay connected in their lives. How do I know? I hear it from them. They demonstrate it through their actions. Even greater, they could have completely gone in a separate direction without ever talking with me again. I call that determination. Determination can be very contagious. Thanks, Little Brothers!

Never Give Up on the Team

More important, through your lifestyle, teach those whom you imbue with a glimpse of enduring until the end. How can young men use their determination to their advantage? It certainly is not always an easy answer for me. However, I realize that I need an equivalent amount of determination in order to assist them with remaining undeterred. Again, the ability to assist young men from becoming discouraged requires influential qualities, wisdom, persistence, honesty and other relevant attributes. When I introduce the term "team determination" to one of my young guys, it is due to various strengths that I have recognized within him.

Some of my mentees are determined to graduate school, start a career, develop skills, rectify past errors and become productive citizens. My job is to help them achieve those goals and assist them on that long life voyage. I usually find myself addressing two questions along this journey. What does it take to become successful? How do I measure their success? Those questions assist me with identifying some specific pieces to the puzzle. This is when I submit to J.D.'s theme ("hard work-work"). When I invest adequate time in preparation, then the results cater to that initial work. It is rewarding to see young men that improve their determination traits with skills such as focus, a strong work ethic, listening attentively and persistence. Some of these young guys present a strong sense of motivation with sports, academics and practical abilities. I do not have any specific formula for bringing out the best in themselves. However, I rely on prayer as my base. I really can tell the difference when I do not pray prior to working with my young guys. My primary job is to accurately identify their strengths so that I can build on the foundation. It would be impossible to enumerate the times when these young men compelled me with their skills, determination, passion and knowledge. I often tell the young guys, "I want to learn just as much from you as you may from me." Furthermore, they are more than willing to teach me. How much do you learn from young people? Reciprocal relationship! By operating with that type of mindset, it puts me in a position to reinforce their determination through my authentic interest in them. The influence of determination can be observed through the influencer's response, availability and personal investment.

See Beyond the Obstacles

Some of the young guys are grappling with a determination to overcome severe emotional family pain. If we pay attention closely, we will observe their struggle. At times you can see it in their eyes. Do you ever think it is unfair for young people to experience life trauma? There is no right or wrong answer. I simply want you to consider that question for your personal thoughts. Over the years, there have been many stories shared with me regarding the hardships experienced from young men. By listening to many stories, I have been able to discern that many issues with young men are not incurred because they were seeking trouble. In a high number of situations, their troubles are related to another source. There are some serious problematic situations facing our youths, but I have never discovered any incorrigible young men in my personal work. God is able to transform the heart. I'm not disheartened by their present obstacles and the severity of their perceived future outcome. But something needs to be done to rearrange the forecast of misery, disrespect, complacency, entitlement, abuse and denial. It starts with you, fathers and mentors. Influence does not discriminate. What type of influence will you pour into young people to make active for their lives? Your ability to compel them in a positive fashion is a conscious choice that needs to be made. If not, then you will need to consider what the outcome may be for the life of that young person.

The fact of the matter is that all of us have a story. Some of us were able to overcome dreadful circumstances. The condition of people matters greatly. Consequently, there are many individuals who have a tendency to pre-judge because they are unwilling to spend time with the hurt individual. Time! It takes a certain heart for humanity to move beyond the surface of the pain of another human being. I must acknowledge in a forthright manner that there are times when some young men appeared to be facing insurmountable life barriers. However, it was only an appearance. So I'm reminded of the many people that were able to excel in the face of an apparition of gloom. As men of influence, we will need to resist acquiescing to those un-influencing moments. Lord, you are my influence.

Become Effective and Efficient

Are you effective regarding most things you strive to achieve in life? This is not a set-up question. It is also not about being right or wrong with your answer. When I was at the equine rescue farm with one of my young guys volunteering, I learned a simple and valuable lesson. What was the lesson? "It is not always about whether something is right or wrong." But we do have an opportunity to become increasingly efficient and effective. I was just minding my business and doing my routine work on the farm on this particular day. The opportunity to spend time with horses is more prevalent in the rural areas as opposed to the city environment in which I grew up. So when this young man, Brother Alex, conveyed ways to do things in an efficient manner I absolutely gave him my attention.

On this day, I learned that even the most simplistic job can become easier to handle through paying attention to a young man willing to take his valuable time to advance my workmanship. This young man taught me to make my volunteer work much easier through utilizing a tool in a more efficient manner. Not only was I more effective at the job, but my relationship with this young stranger became increasingly strengthened. Coincidently, this same young man approached me on a different day and told me that he appreciated the work that I do with young men. I thank God for the powerful subtle messages that come to life in the most noisy, smelly and labor-intensive times. Being influenced by young people can be very humbling, especially when it deals with challenging labor as opposed to technology. Many young people are really good at enlightening me with technology due to my lack of technological savvy. I will take all positive influences from young men especially when it occurs in an abnormal relationship, uncanny environment and against all odds. Lord, your purpose is clear for our lives, so help us to look beyond the dust, filth and pain that attempt to cloud our vision

I really enjoy the concept of passing influences on to the next person. When I work with young men, I think it is critical to join with them in teamwork instead of making them do something without participating. Working alongside them in a tenacious manner has delivered great team dividends in my rapport with young men. I also think exposing young men to relevant volunteer opportunities assist them with gaining new life possibilities. However, if we understand the power of influence then you will observe that it can occur at some of the strangest times. But we can become increasingly efficient by just paying attention to the valuable insight of others.

Take Care of Your Body

My cousin, Dawn, was a great motivator for assisting me to transform my health over three years ago. She became an unofficial doctor for me. I dealt with having several headaches a month for more than 20 years because of eating habits related to hypertension. Initially, I thought my headaches were a result of boxing. In all those years, I do not recall any of my doctors emphatically expressing the importance of reading packaged food labels and substantially reducing sodium intake. I remember the unexpected call from my cousin in Philly in May 2012 as she passionately conveyed her thoughts in a cogent manner to modify my diet. She made it clear that educating myself on sodium intake could be helpful to my health and eliminate my headaches. The rest is history. For three years, my blood pressure consistently reads great, according to the doctors and blood pressure machines at local stores. In addition, I have not experienced headaches subsequent to changing my diet and continuing to exercise on a regular basis. As a result, I have not taken any medicine over the past three years related to headaches.

I'm not putting down any doctors, because I have experienced some great help from them. But your opportunity for a transformed life may come from an ordinary family member who cares enormously about your wellbeing. Mostly, influence comes from those you trust in life. We all benefit from listening and applying techniques that align with living a healthy life. In my opinion, there is not too much that compares to living healthy daily. When you become free of a very long burden, it feels like a second chance at life. I'm so grateful for being renewed and restored in my physical health. Do not allow selfishness or other perceived inadequacies to preclude you from passing on potential positive life-altering insight to a loved one, friend or even an enemy. Cousin (Dawn) will always be Dr. Dawn and so much more to me.

Now, my renewed focus in family life, business and ministry supersedes my previous headache-induced years. I'm not complaining, but it makes such a difference when you are not limited in your life endeavors and passion by intrusive factors. Furthermore, information that is conducive to your prosperity and peace may arrive when you least expect it. In too many circumstances, we find ourselves taking care of cars and other superficial items prior to attending to personal wellbeing. Many of us are guilty of it. I do not have the statistics, but I have continuously heard that men are more negligent about going to doctors for check-ups compared to women. Nevertheless, influence will not be possible or only partially effective if you are not invested in taking care of yourself. When you are in a position to thrive, then enhance it with discipline, consistency, action and perpetually trusting God for the long haul.

CHAPTER 14

✳✳✳

Give It Time

Do Not Be Too Hasty

WITH TIME, MANY things can be overcome. If you made minor, moderate or major errors in your life, they do not equate to your demise. In addition, I become concerned with individuals who are too impatient to wait and instead attempt to intercede in situations in an untimely fashion. Many terrible life-deteriorating situations occur because people are undisciplined and unprepared to eradicate rage before tragedy strikes. Allow time to be a healer. Avoid regrets and give situations time while using God's wisdom prior to confronting unstable situations. We can use the advantage of patience in most of our life dealings and relationships. *Urge the older men to be temperate, venerable (serious), sensible, self-controlled, and sound in the faith, in the love, and in the steadfastness and patience [of Christ] (Titus 2:2).*

Once time does its work, now you can approach with emotions in check. Unfortunately, some fathers do not have the privilege of influencing their sons in person, because some men have prematurely approached adversity with bad timing. In many cases, being absent in the lives of our sons will require more than one significant visit or interaction with them. We need to become increasingly aware of earning their hearts and developing trustworthiness over time. Brothers, we could potentially leave our children in an empty situation if we do not move with purpose intertwined with good timing.

Therefore, you will benefit from addressing effective leadership, correction and being shaped with the heart of a family man. I encourage you to study God's word regarding the purpose of men in the family, community and your role as the head of the household. In time, I deeply trust that we can revamp, revive and re-strengthen family dynamics. I believe in you, brother, and more important, God desires the family to prosper.

Ready Yourself to be Influenced

The ability to influence is not always an easy process and demands determination to accomplish the task. Whether you are the influencer or the one being influenced, there is work involved by each individual. It takes time and energy to become effective with compelling others. Conversely, not everyone is ready to be influenced. Timing is everything. How do you predict when a person is ready to be influenced? This is an important question to ask.

If you think influencing is a matter of conveying your qualities, message and gifts without understanding the recipient of your influence, then you are mistaken. Too many times, we become riveted with telling our story and never take the time to understand the story of others. I like to say, "You need to be receptive to being influenced before you attempt to influence someone." Are there people you should *not* influence? Consider your influencing results. Realistically, I can relate to not wanting to be influenced as a young man because of selfishness and other regretful desires to remain stuck in life. So it is not necessarily a personal attack against you if people are unwilling to be influenced or adhere to your guidance. There are simply some individuals who are not willing to surrender, even when it is for their own good. Make sure you understand the difference.

In other situations, it is not the young person but the adult struggling with making the necessary changes to affect his household. As adults, we can be more resistant to becoming free of conflict and other salient problematic situations. Why? Well, you need to honestly answer that question based on your personal distractions. I can only speak about my obstacles regarding the various shortcomings encountered in my journey. As a professional and family man, I have learned that oftentimes we already have the solution to our problems. The real problem comes down to some blockage with seeing the answer right in front of you. Do you ever experience having the resolution to your problems but never use them? Any blockage, such as ego, controlling ways, self-rogue, self-loathing and misery will constantly inhibit progress. Lord, if I refuse to concede to Your ways, then even retaining the right answer is a futile influence.

Become Un-stuck

One of the main things that inhibited me from influencing myself and others was the feeling of being stuck. This can take on many forms, such as a lack of resources, reticence, distrust, bad experiences, faithless approaches…the list can be unending. When facing these stuck times, the objective is always to become un-stuck. Contingent on the severity of the circumstances, it will take longer to handle some of our stuck situations. I want to encourage all of us to always be sufficiently transparent with ourselves to move through the quagmires and crucibles. In life, we will encounter uncomfortable and inescapable crises. Confront them! It is only part of the life journey to experience trials, crises and calamities. You are familiar with the saying, "Whatever dos not kill you makes you stronger." Well, I say, "You have the ability to become strengthened through the Source in your life."

At times, J.D. has moments when he feels stuck and attempts to give up when facing adverse situations. There are times when I give him ample time to work through difficulties. On other occasions, I empower him in a creative way to become un-stuck. It typically means building his confidence with words to assist him with self-assurance. Other times, it is not so easy. He may need me to assure him that he is capable of achieving a goal. Therefore, assisting him with writing the alphabet, building Lego towers, doing head stands, hanging from exercise equipment and various hands-on moments with Daddy increases his self-confidence. Being aware of what it takes to encourage our sons heightens the bond between father and son.

Mentor Through Difficult Experiences

I do not think anything will exceed the lost feeling of a young person dying that you were connected with for some duration. It did not occur many times, but I have experienced the death of a former mentee. Unfortunately, one of my former young guys lost his life tragically while experimenting with illicit drugs. Although I was no longer in his life, it was a painful experience to undertake. So it continues to be imperative to value our young people and not neglect the power of influence because we think there is time. Be efficient! I encourage you to trust and respond to the Holy Spirit leading you to take action.

I wrestle with various challenging situations in my work with young men. Once I develop a strong rapport with them, it feels personal if they do not reach their potential. I reflect on a number of young men whom I hope overcome the traps of life. I believe there are young men who can become college students, great husbands, leaders, entrepreneurs and powerful men of God. Never give up! God has the final answer. I want for them the same that I aspire for my children.

I recognize the importance of influence, but persuading young men to transition their skills into real life is typically not an easy task. I acknowledge that this remains an area for my personal growth and development. Networking with other solid resourceful individuals continues to be an impetus for my successful mentoring. I greatly appreciate other leaders dedicated to the lives of young men. I frequently remind myself that I do not have to know everything, and connecting with the right people reduces the pressure to know it all. In addition, I hold onto important personal sayings, such as, "No quitting allowed." That is why influence is not for the faint of heart. It is for those willing to keep their hearts invested in the young person, especially when you feel faint. *But they that wait upon the Lord shall renew their strength; they shall mount up with wings as eagles; they shall run, and not be weary; and they shall walk, and not faint (Isaiah 40:31).*

Strive for Longevity

I do trust that some relationships are only meant for a temporary duration. But I also understand there are many relationships that have been deflated because some individuals lack a longevity perspective. I acknowledge losing perspective on occasions about the significance of longevity, and I made unwise errors in some circumstances. Use prudence to understand the purpose of your pursuits, especially regarding relationships and other goals. Longevity for some tasks will require increased commitment, quality time, resources, sacrifice, humility and a high level of selflessness. As a result, many will abandon the race far before reaching the finish line. Think on these next thoughts.

There are situations when young people struggle in relationships because adults make unfulfilled promises. I'm not mentioning these thoughts to make you ashamed or embarrassed about past errors. We all make errors, and that is a part of life. However, it should not be acceptable to avoid working on poor habits. In addition, we are only as good as our word to others. In particular, young people know when they can no longer trust you at your word. The ability to have longevity in our connection and influence with youths could be determined through our diligent communication with them.

My focus is mainly regarding the needs of our children and young people. So keep your word or do not give it. We all understand things happen to prevent follow-through, but mostly I encourage us to walk and live in integrity. Influence matters, and there is a substantial amount of empty influence being regurgitated by leaders. As a result, young people learn not to trust, or they are left with some feeling of insecurity. Overcoming those deficiencies could be very tedious for all involved in the process. We should be careful to avoid leaving our children in a state of vacuity and uncertainty. Longevity rules!

How do we improve in our longevity perspective? Think beyond the minutiae and become acquainted with the greater goal. In other words, use whatever helps you to rise above short-term thinking and premature responses. The long-view perspective brings benefits, such as dependability, accountability, trust and hope. When we operate from those particular attributes, other people become the recipients of our committed action.

When you demonstrate care toward young men, then it will be obvious to them. I think about two young men, Brother John and Brother Darius in particular who through prayer I was able to develop a rapport that empowered our ongoing achievements. There are certain young men who will make you earn their time, respect and friendship. I find it amazing when young men are not interested in having a male leader in their lives for various reasons, and the Lord selects you to transform their position. I'm grateful for God's calling on my life regarding working with young men, but the responsibility is on me to further develop my gift. Although the Lord will not abandon me, I still have a great measure of work to accomplish for the greater goals with young men. In all my influential relationships (long term and short term) with young men, I have been influenced for a lifetime. Keep believing, brothers!

Furthermore, men should never undervalue the privilege of reaching young men who otherwise would be unreachable. I have observed young men benefit from a long-term relationship with a trustworthy man. In these auspicious relationships, the parameters of distrust have dissipated in the young man's heart toward that particular man. You have an advantage that other men will not be privileged to experience. However, it can be a very fragile place for young men that could easily be broken without the proper follow-through, commitment and wisdom of God. When we are able to break through the shield of insecurity with young men, then it is worthwhile to honor, support and increase our spiritual quest for ongoing effectiveness. At times, the *lack* of continuity can be destructive toward long-term endeavors. Make it easy, and reduce the complexities of your flow with young men. In other words, stop putting all the trust in your restricted abilities. Go deeper with the Lord for the purpose of the long haul.

The deeper part is the responsibility that goes with becoming the trusting male in a young man's life. As the Lord gives men the responsibility to be that important man toward young men, then we should not take it lightly or move in our own strength. Some of these young men have been so disappointed over the years from the non-commitment of men. The wedge of distrust becomes thicker, if they give their hearts only to be let down by another positive male figure. Therefore, it will be crucial for men to understand the influence they hold over the lives of young men. I consider influencing from a longevity perspective as the most pivotal influence.

Why? You hold the power to influencing them at an unprecedented plateau. In my experience, young men who absolutely know you care for them continue to seek you out for many years to come. I do not take that for granted.

In fact, I'm extremely grateful for several young men who started with me as teenagers and continue to connect with me as married men and family men. Personally, there is no substitute for being able to pray with those young men and listen to the various inquiries they express about developing their faith. Yet I still have a great deal of work to do for greater impact, constant preparation and guidance of young men. Furthermore, it is certainly an area that I yearn for more of God's wisdom and aspire to obey for ongoing effective results with young men.

Longevity influence covers our ability to teach from a spiritual, practical, and natural standpoint. It really is a comprehensive endeavor that requires men to address some formidable issues in order to equip young men with knowledge and pragmatic goals. We will discover that some of these impressionable young men need guidance with learning new ways to treat females in a respectful manner. Other young guys are struggling with ways to understand a life with purpose. I have encountered situations when young men are lost because of a spiritual deficiency. Another challenging area concerns many young men dealing with some pain that occurred in their early years. How do we begin to help our young men? They need our time, commitment, love, courage, strength and hope. Therefore, the ability to spend a long time with young men when feasible demands great accountability.

Remember, when you really have an unconditional love and care for these young men, it carries significant meaning in their lives. Do not lose the ability to influence because you get tangled up with your limited version of influence—at least that happened to me at one point. Now, I recognize clearly that the Lord gives us precisely what we need to handle every life circumstance. *For everyone to whom much is given, of him shall much be required; and of him to whom men entrust much, they will require and demand all the more (Luke 12:48).* Furthermore, responsibility will not automatically become easy because you trust the Lord. For me, the greater responsibility means that I will need Him even more to complete the tasks in front of me. In some cases, we have all that is needed to get the job done, but we still need to be vigilant throughout the voyage. In addition, there are a multitude of times when you will be able to connect young men with other essential resources to assist them with real-life situations. So I refer to longevity influence as a time to seek God for identifying needs, remaining courageous, enduring strength, applying His word and getting the job done.

Remain Influential for Longevity of Your Actions or Career

When people have done things for a long duration, it does not necessarily mean they are proficient. Have you ever heard people mention the following words? "I have been doing this for the past 20 years, so it makes me an expert." It does not mean you are doing it right or better than other people. One can easily become misled into thinking that long duration equates automatic truth. Think about this! Do you know someone who never grows in his or her career despite doing it for an extremely long time? My point is to not take your copious amount of years in a career and use it as a weapon to wave in the face of others. It may be a malfunctioned weapon.

The ability to remain consistent at something certainly deserves recognition. However, influence can become stagnate or non-existent without understanding our purpose, development and position. Truthfully, there are people that can be involved for long periods of time and never make a difference. Mostly, they become satisfied with a personal goal of "being there" until their time is up. How do I know? You can tell by the lack of investment in attitude, customer service, passion, courtesy and other missing attributes. The ability to accomplish longevity with someone becomes impotent, if our influence makes other people feel they would rather avoid our presence. Do not place yourself above other individuals because you have more experience. Your excessive time spent in your career does not always qualify you as the most appropriate person for the job. Please remain humble; influence that drowns itself in *despot* behavior is referred to as tyranny.

How long have you been involved in your career? What do people experience when they leave your company? People will absolutely let you know what they think about you. Are you doing it just to pass the time until retirement? Re-evaluate! Re-assess! When we spend time genuinely working on our character, passion, goals, thoughts, relationships and life qualities, then we can move in a more prosperous fashion. Examine yourself! Longevity does not mean we are not replaceable. But it does mean we are equipped to potentially influence in an informative, encouraging and trustworthy manner. Do not allow the flaws, inconsistencies and insecurities of others to destroy God's durability within you.

Influence by Repetition

Have you ever been persuaded because you heard positive things mentioned to you on a daily basis, for example, a trustworthy person constantly encouraging you that one day success will come your way? It is a good feeling when you become accustomed to hearing those promising words from a person invested in your best welfare. You will probably believe it at some point, even if you were reticent about some aspects of your life. The ability to hear positive influence by a noble, honorable and trustworthy individual is valuable. So J.D. and Daddy have this influence by repetition that we practice during our sports activities at home. I did not notice the impact this particular repetitive activity was having on J.D. until I listened to him playing by himself in the kitchen. I was cooking at the time and he was repeating the words of influence that I undertake with him. When J.D. does well at basketball, play boxing, football or other games, then I will put him on my shoulders and shout loudly that he is the champion. I will say his full name and raise his hands in the air announcing "champion of the world" while running around with him on my shoulders. He loves it enormously. Appropriately, he reciprocates the behavior to me. He asks me to get on his little shoulders while he declares that Daddy is also the champion. Many fathers can relate to making their sons the newly crowned champion. It is something that I learned from my boxing days, and I apply them in a fun way with my son. I should not be surprised that influence by repetition could occur even when J.D. is using his imagination and playing all by himself.

I believe the contrary can exist as well. If we are constantly told demeaning things about ourselves, it is disastrous for us, in particular, parents, leaders and those in authority expressing denigrating words to their children, supporters, followers or subordinates. During the most frustrating times, the ability to restrain from communicating painful words is important. We benefit from using techniques that will prevent us from conveying regrettable words. Words are spontaneous. Once you say them, you are not able to retrieve them nor will they vanish in thin air. How do we handle these challenging situations? We will not always have the privilege of walking away from a heated situation. However, I recognize it is not about being perfect but identifying, planning and executing situations in a better way. Well, I go back to recognizing my limits. There are just some things that are impossible without God's help. I love passing my burdens to the Lord, because it allows me to recapture my peace. Furthermore, we should expect challenges, issues and hardships in this life journey. So do not fall under the illusion that God will remove every test from our lives. Most people do not want to be told things that are harmful to their lives, but I trust the fragile-hearted individual struggles even more through negative words of influence.

I recently heard a gentleman on the radio encourage parents to beat their children. I know this is a moot subject, and I want you to ruminate on the influence of physical discipline. The same man mentioned that beatings blessed his life. I will not debate him on what he feels blessed his life. But let me ask this question. If you have ever been beaten or currently beat your child, why does it get to that point? Is it because of the child? Is it because of the parent being depleted of his patience? Is it a combination of these? Furthermore, do we think anything subtle occurs between parents and their children subsequent to physical discipline? I will not attempt to tell anyone how to raise their children. In addition, it is not about making parents revisit their past faults and making them feel bad. How do you view conveying negative things every time you get frustrated with your child? Does negative verbal influence impact our children? We are usually quick to become sensitive to other people expressing negative verbalizations or physical aggression toward our children as well as toward ourselves. Correct? We do not tolerate it from others, but is it necessary for us to do it to others, especially our children?

I'm initiating thought on this subject and suggest that you reflect on it in an earnest manner. I enjoy the difficult reflection when we approach it from an inward perspective. I understand this is a personal situation, and that is why I'm mentioning it. For the record, I have made plenty of errors in my parenting style, so I'm not speaking from a pretentious platform. My goal is to point us in the direction of assessing our influence at a deeper level. I will only interject my experience, progress and thoughts regarding physical discipline with my children. The experience for me to restrain from physical discipline has been rewarding, especially concerning the rapport with my children. It is not perfect, but it has its benefits. When I take an introspective look at physical discipline, then it causes me to look at this one thing. The times when I want to physically discipline my children are when I'm out of control, frustrated and lacking patience. I'm just being forthright regarding my thoughts, feelings and position with physical discipline. Therefore, I concluded that it is necessary for me to deal with me much better as an effective parent and go from there. Some people will agree with being hands-free with their children, and others will disagree. Great! Of course, every parent is entitled to their style of discipline. Does it mean that each parent who physically disciplines is a terrible leader? I certainly do not believe that about parents. In fact, a lack of physical discipline does not mean our children will do most things right. But I do trust that a comprehensive understanding of God's word pertaining to raising our children puts us in a position to deliver the best influence.

Influence Through Fun

"Can we do the spider man puzzle?" J.D. has not yet mastered ways to figure out jigsaw puzzles. But he puts in effort, and he will stick next to Daddy until the puzzle is completed. Did I mention that jigsaw puzzles can become a competitive game when it comes to J.D.? Like father, like son! The ability to put together 100-piece jigsaw puzzles with J.D. is not easy. Azaria usually assists us with putting puzzles together. She is a quasi-pro with these small puzzles. It became clear to me from watching a few families do jigsaw puzzles as a unit that it was an opportunity to spend quality time together—not just ordinary time but fun, educational and loving time together. You discern the type of time needed with your family. If we are going to influence at the highest level with our children, then we will find it essential to become flexible with our time. Yes, fathers will need to make a sacrifice with their time for the simplest events. I celebrate the many families who take advantage of their quality time together. In most scenarios, I have enough patience to work on puzzles with my children. However, it is not my forte. I have grown to enjoy the learning experience, patience, organization, focus and creativity it takes to start and finish jigsaw puzzles. Mostly, I have become accustomed to watching my two youngest children think intensely, laugh, compete and collaborate with Daddy for a common goal: The influence of pleasurable times!

What is your common goal with your children? You can engage them with chess, checkers, cards, monopoly, basketball, tennis, jump rope and video games. The ability to bring hope to the life of another far exceeds the particular game you play. More important, consider the ultimate goal that God desires for you and the person being influenced. If you missed the purpose between you and the one being influenced, then it could diminish the outcome. It does not mean there must be some substantial plan or scheme. Just make an impact!

My ability to influence absolutely requires prayer, integrity, patience, research, love, compassion and truth. I notice the difference when I do not enhance my personal qualities and approach situations without any real substance. It is not a pretty situation. Also, those being influenced become the recipients of my residue or secondary work when I decide to give less of myself. There are other times when listening is a necessary *facet* to achieving my goals. Self-control is a major ingredient for my success in all relationships. *But the fruit of the [Holy] Spirit [the work which His presence within accomplishes] is love, joy (gladness), peace, patience (an even temper, forbearance), kindness, goodness (benevolence), faithfulness, Gentleness (meekness, humility), self-control (self-restraint, continence). Against such things there is no law (that can bring a charge) (Galatians 5:22-23).*

The increased level of time spent with influencing J.D. continues to evolve into a more in-depth familiarity with him. In addition, positive habit development becomes second nature for both of us when Daddy approaches life with a passion. It really is a reciprocal relationship. The more we invest in our sons with God's wisdom, the more you can expect *equivalent* returns. Let me remind us of one important factor. The consistency necessary with positive habit development can be elusive without daily persistence, adjustments and taking action. When an individual influences with consistent integrity, truth and positive qualities then the message you convey will hold its own weight.

Of course this rapport is not exclusive to father and son influence. The collaborative influence can include various combinations. Uncle and neice! Aunt and nephew! Mother and son! Grandfather and grandchild! Teacher and student! You get the picture. Anybody willing to invest time and other essential attributes will be in a position to make an impact. There are no parameters, boundaries or limitations for making your goal come alive during the father and son influence, as well as other compelling relationships. If you use a puzzle or some other method to engage youngsters, your effect will exponentially increase with unconditional love for the individual. I frequently say, "There are so many things that are impossible to achieve in my life without yielding to the Lord's plan." This includes being a husband, father or mentor of substance. It is not possible for me to flourish in any of these roles without understanding that God is in control. I actually love knowing that God is in control, because it makes life enjoyable. Try trusting Jesus!

Follow Up

Anyone could be successful as an influential person when it comes to follow up. Let me use J.D. as an example to make my point clear. It really impresses me with the things that children remember when it is advantageous for them. They call it "selective memory," and children are the best at it. Conversely, remembering homework and chores seem to escape this category of selective memory for some children. There are times we have to laugh at our children because they remind us of ourselves. I think my mother warned me that I would experience some tough days in parenting. My son actually helps me with follow-up because he constantly says, "Daddy you said you were going to do 'this' and 'that with me." Miraculously, he remembers every detail and each event that I promised to do with him. It really is critical to keep our word and follow up consistently. Follow up with even minor events and situations carry significant weight pertaining to our children regardless of their age.

Follow-up means you have the ability to influence through reliability, trust and unequivocally that you mean what you say. Although that does not appear to require a special skill, it really expresses the earnest approach in one's heart. Follow-up also puts other people in a position to feel secure and relaxed knowing that you are a man of your word. We absolutely need this simple means of practicing good habits in all relationships, but I trust practicing this habit at home delivers the greatest value. What do you need to follow up on? Think before you commit, especially to children. If not, you may find yourself making excuses due to your initial insincerity with your original word. Do not oversimplify nor undervalue the importance of follow-up. Work on practicing your follow-through, and you will undoubtedly make progress in your pursuits and exemplary practice with influenced individuals.

Too many times we have backed ourselves in a corner by speaking without thinking. In the future, value the feelings of others before speaking in a loose and impractical manner. In addition, a lack of follow-up can translate into an unscrupulous mindset, apathy, dishonesty or animosity, to name several defects of character.

— ✳✳✳ —

Regroup

One more Round

LET ME USE boxing as an analogy to clarify the regroup perspective. There are times when being hit as a boxer exposes your character, desire and heart. Consequently, the toughest fighter can be hit in a certain spot and it is a done deal. So I express to us that regrouping as fathers will take determination, effort, courage and commitment. Your potential to compel your son may be contingent on your diligence at "mixing it up" with your greatest adversary. Identifying the opponents in your life is beneficial for learning ways to effectively work toward healing and peace. If you have multiple adversaries, it only means victory will be exponentially greater.

I'm encouraged by husbands, because we are the leaders of the family. The family will remain "on the canvas" unless men continue training, overcoming and going the entire distance as courageous fighters for the household. If you are already down, you are still not "out for the count." It means you are in a position to regroup. Some fathers are metaphorically healing from bloody noses, black eyes and sore ribs. The last time I checked, Scripture reminded me that Jesus was wounded for our transgressions and bruised for our iniquities. Your peace and serenity are not far away. Stop precluding yourself from raising your hands in victory. Get up and regroup! Afterward, go and get some other father off the canvas of life. The power to influence through regrouping is a self-motivator, which lends itself to some of the greatest supports during unprecedented moments. I'm grateful for the word of the Lord, which moves me forward during the times of solitude. Keep regrouping, brothers, for you are not alone, even when you are by yourself.

Get Off the Canvas of Life

I'm so grateful for the men that God has placed in my life. I really learned to value ways to assist men with getting off the canvas of life while gaining so much from the young men entrusted to me. My particular style is to learn from family men as much as possible while assisting them to move beyond family obstacles and challenges. I recall having two positive family men seeking some guidance from me as we confronted some difficult issues. I'm still flabbergasted at how these same men were encouraging and empowering to me for months as we met together to work through challenges. If you pay close attention, you will potentially find the message God is giving you through the lives of others. Never allow yourself to become self-righteous and forget that you may be close to landing on the canvas of life. There are things that I'm better equipped to handle because I have been influenced by the stories of others. We can avoid many traps and failures through disciplined obedience, faithfulness and the practical advice of a friend. Brothers, let us continue to support each other.

I recognized at least two important factors about becoming prepared and equipped as a family man through wise counsel. First, it definitively requires ongoing work as a family man. Secondly, it is vitally important to live out the things you teach. The ability to influence other men will depend on your credibility as a leader within your own home. In fact, I remember vividly hearing a respected leader mention. "We should not preach what we do not believe ourselves." You will come off as insincere, implausible and unreliable.

For years now, I have perceived myself as a leader of young men who have been troubled by life. Young men facing difficult situations are my forte group. But it does not mean God limits me to one dimension of work among men. So when I received a call from two men regarding assisting them through family obstacles, it was time to revisit the things the Lord was equipping me to accomplish. Influence may come from your ability to do something with integrity now that was once an impediment in your personal life.

Allow for Surprise Influences

Influence can come in an astonishing manner especially when you are not anticipating learning things that already appear palpable. You never know when, where or who can give you influence, if you are amenable to gaining new insight. When can you be influenced? Influence can arrive at a time when you least expect it. Remember, influence can derive from the practical, spiritual, emotional or physical areas of life. God's wisdom will enable you to know what to retain for your life. The ability to become influenced in the unforeseen times can be some of the most meaningful influences. Why? When you think there was nothing meaningful to learn and you discover otherwise, then it could have a lasting or immediate impact. Where can you be influenced? It can occur in a room that is filled with scholars or some of the ordinary people within the crowd. The beauty about both influences comes from the weight, significance, meaning and hope that both influences deliver to your life.

In my estimation, one must remove and replace any arrogant attitudes in order to become affected by those whom you may not expect to give profound advice. Rid your life of improvident, judgmental, pompous and presumptuous approaches toward others. Who can influence you? Nobody or anybody! Both answers are correct. It totally depends on you. Nobody can influence you when you are unwilling to become influenced. There are many people who have lost their sense of hope, passion or determination. Conversely, anybody can compel you when you value people based on God's capability of using whomever he declares suitable to convey an inspiring message to your life. Listen for discernment, truth and purpose. Be watchful of the "anybody" of life, because he or she may be precisely that person who transforms your perspective.

Use Positive Potential

Do you ever consider the amount of potential in your life? I classify potential as the ability to experience talents and gifts, especially reserved for the purpose of future use. Similarly, it is hope that empowers us to not become exhausted by our current or overwhelming circumstances, because there is something greater within us. This could be a motivator for all of us. Even when things are going well, I want to trust God regarding potential and its connection to my life. Too many times complacency replaces our determination and unfulfilled promises. You have an abundance of potential, and I hope it compels you to do something positive.

I remember listening to a few professors from two separate colleges express the significance of researching, studying and becoming an expert in your field. Both professors discussed having bosses who were not more college educated than they. In fact, one of them had a boss without a college education. But their bosses were experts in their field. I think J.D. would tell all of us that hard work-work brings many benefits despite the lack of credentials. The influence of potential is not reduced to the awards on the wall; instead it will not become constrained by the walls amid your life.

I have encountered many young men who are much better than me with building, fixing and understanding technical information. These guys have potential as teenagers. Many times we take our talents for granted. Therefore, I encourage those young men to pursue the things that come easy and are enjoyable to them. Most of us have heard it expressed that having a job we enjoy makes it feel like we are not really working at all. In addition, learning your craft at an early age will expose your potential and give you the advantage of optimizing your life calling. Allow your potential to work for you through shaping it, trusting it and at times going against the popular choices. You are unique, so let your potential express a distinguished, honorable, noble and determined man of God.

Many people will never be on your side unless they are able to get something from you. Those are superficial friends, and I like to keep my distance from them. In addition, I gain new potential when I witness my young mentees accomplish something for the first time. I begin to understand more clearly that being a part of their experience will help them fortify their confidence about what they are capable of achieving. The ability to help others reach their potential may help you attain a renewed viable potential as well.

Be Studious

I trust there needs to be an emphasis on our willingness to become studious and not only presenting a desire to teach others. Some people only want to be in charge without being "charged" by others. I trust this is a major mistake, even if you are successful with doing things on your own. At the minimum, I certainly understand that earnest prayer will point you in the right direction. You may not always desire to collaborate with others, but being studious is an enormous asset. Furthermore, I think the best teachers are simultaneously the best students. So I'm capable of influencing the lives of young men when I yield to personal mentors who lead me in a spiritual, natural and pragmatic fashion. Remember, leadership really matters. In many circumstances, we will find that following the proper order empowers us to become effective with the task in front of us. When you take time to become increasingly studious in your professional, recreational and personal life, then consider the other important areas, too.

Brothers, how studious are you in your marital life? I trust there are many men who are very attentive, studious and successful when it comes to understanding their wives. So I do not want to exclude those great leading men among us. I think there are valuable lessons many of us can learn from those men, and I'm no exception. Primarily, I'm looking at the way we can consistently demonstrate an influence that is incomparable in its principles. Influencing our wives through our demonstration of love, kindness, gentleness, courage and prayer brings sound results. I have seen positive results from working on those paramount spiritual components, but I certainly have room to grow in some of these virtues. What about you, brother? Do not be deceived, we are the essential leaders in our homes. What will happen if we do not begin to influence in the proper manner? Maybe some of the same things or potentially it will become worse. I'm thinking the latter will be the greater possibility. There is no way for me to measure up to being a man of influence at the highest echelon without implementing those principles consistently in my own home. When I do things according to my own direction, it usually has a short shelf life. In addition, there is much to be gained as a result of a husband influencing with the proper array, values and purpose. We will not only benefit our family dynamics, but specifically we put our sons in a position to gain valuable assets as a future loving husband and family man. Influence is not only a matter of considering the impact you are incurring in one individual. But influence with a long duration objective also takes a long look at the ensuing generational effect.

Value Others as Yourself

And straightway the father of the child cried out, and said with tears, Lord, I believe; help thou mine unbelief (Mark 9:24). In my assessment, one of the reasons we devalue others is due to our questionable trust and belief. The value of others is contingent on how we picture them. Allow me to use the topic of marriage to convey my thoughts. In your marriage, you are not less than who you were during the early stages. Similarly, your wife still carries the same appeal from 20 years ago. We all understand that physical looks will dissipate at some point. However, if you got married to your spouse strictly based on the physical and no other substantive connection, then your value was established on a broken foundation. You were influenced by an incomplete, empty and short-sighted motivation. As a result, it derails you from consistently experiencing what the Lord promised for you and your spouse regarding His unblemished covenant. You can still get back on track. Your original purpose, perspective, language and treatment, became disoriented and lost during the subsequent stages. However, the ongoing value should be coated with the truth of God's intention for your marriage. I'm not aware of any greater practical knowledge to ensure the highest premium thoughts regarding the value of my bride and success for other married couples.

It does not mean all challenges and obstacles fade away in your relationship because of positive thoughts. But labeling others with a positive value combined with godly thoughts enables you to be cognizant of reducing others to a valueless position. Why do we decrease our value in relationships with spouses, friends, family and other individuals? It would be irresponsible to suggest one uniform answer for each situation. I would say with some sense of certainty that it is essential to watch our value meter in all relationships. If you have reduced an individual to a lower value, take time to evaluate and execute on modifying your actions. Immediately! Even the best marriages need to make adjustments, reassess and unceasingly put in work. Negative thinking will creep in at unguarded moments. Let us remember the way we formerly envisioned our spouses with only the highest quality. Did your thoughts of your spouse reduce themselves to a "value burger mentality," connection and purpose? Do something about it before it deteriorates into a completely unwholesome value.

Why does premium value matter with all relationships? When you begin to devalue people because of their errors, flaws and imperfections, then it shatters your potential influence on them. Why? You will subconsciously make them inadequate, irrelevant and unworthy of your best. Realistically, you are actually reducing your own good character. Learn ways to separate your value of others compared to the personal issues, deficiencies and other character flaws observed in them. If you constantly entertain the thoughts of becoming grossly entangled in decreasing the value of others, it only submerges you beneath the surface of liberty, peace and contentment. You will not only use that type of defective thinking for handling a problematic relationship, but additional dysfunctional thoughts will ensue.

The value of an individual should never be misaligned because of personal vendettas, jealousy or misinformation. You may not have the best rapport with an individual, but always harbor a premium value regarding all people. Your value, outlook and perspective counts! It is paramount to discern whether you view people with the correct lens of life. What lens? Your personal lens empowers you to rise above the lower points about a particular individual into a reestablished image. So I understand that my premium value and influence regarding others rest in working at moving beyond the salient troubled condition of another—not always easy. But it is all a matter of your value lens. However, I trust my confidence in the transformation and greatest value of others will be ongoing for one main reason. Because the Lord was able to transform my life, then anybody can be changed. I rest my case.

Focus Properly on Others

There are many people who are enveloped by a concentration on the bad things of life instead of transitioning their focus on the good. What is the saying? "Misery loves company." The portrayal you have in life will affect those you influence. So I would rather express uplifting thoughts. Peace loves company. Joy loves company. Truth loves company. Your influence will be determined by your perspective on life. If you continually present positivity, it will be conveyed in that manner toward others. We are not able to control the thoughts of anyone else. Don't waste your time. In fact, I never want people to change because of me. That will result in a temporary change. I want to be the bridge in leading the fickle mindset to a mentality of liberation. I encourage us to earnestly strive to become courageous in the most capricious circumstances confronting us. Influence is not just a willingness to correct the errors of other individuals but the heart to admit when you need self-correction.

There are times when people become troubled because they want to make others think or behave like them. In other words, they want to control the lives of others. Do not dismiss this point. Many of us fail in this area and do not realize our controlling ways. One solution: Control *your* life, and other important areas in your life will be better managed. If you are not in control of your focus, then you will remain bothered by the thoughts of others. What is your focus? Influence is not a matter of force but a matter of focus. The Lord does not force us to do anything. He gives us all the essential values to focus on in life. Primarily love! *And now abideth faith, hope, charity, these three; but the greatest of these is charity (1 Corinthians 13:13).*

There were some questions that I routinely ask parents when I began working with their sons. Usually, it does not take long before some parents would follow a pattern of answers that I had heard in the past. During my initial session with a young man, I would request that the parent(s) and son meet with me in my office or at their home. In the first few minutes, I typically ask the following question: "Can you tell me about your son?" I say an extremely high number of parents expressed negative ideas about their sons prior to acknowledging good things about them. Then I changed my line of questioning. "Can you start with the positive qualities that you see in your son?" It would not take long in many circumstances where parents convey a few positive attributes and then begin again discussing all the malfeasance regarding their child.

There are different reasons for this expression of negativity mentioned by parents. No parent should be painted with the same negligence brush despite the commonalities in parenting errors. It does not mean they are terrible parents. It also does not signify that they have "quit" on their sons. In some cases, I certainly think the ongoing obstacles with their sons caused them to identify them as the problem. Conversely, I have constantly been encouraged to hear many parents forwardly express their love for their children. In addition, some well-intentioned parents have already attempted to discover an answer to their dilemma within the home. For example, they may contemplate, "Do I let him live in my home or with his father?" We all understand things happen that destroy the foundation of the home. Brothers, I only hope that we can understand the value of starting, maintaining and enduring to the end with our wives and children.

Furthermore, working with a copious amount of mothers, it is clear they are seeking substantial help for their sons. What needs to be done? Of course, it depends on the needs of the family situation. However, I also understand the wholeness of the family is contingent on the spiritual, practical and daily leadership of a husband. Wives are equally important in the success of the family, and they should not be reduced to an immaterial role. Let me give us a word of value that demands significant application to your situation. If there is a broken person (spouse) within your family dynamics, then do not relegate the merit of your spouse to a meaningless position, especially in front of the children.

Do we need to change our line of thinking? Why do we dwell on the negative so much? Is it a self-portrayal? Do we first think negatively about our children? I will allow you to ruminate on those questions at your convenience. By the way, your son does not have to be a troubled young man in order for you to think negatively about him. I see it all the time in our daily encounters with parents and their children. The ability to control our thinking is critical in averting similar misbehaviors injected into our children. I rely tremendously on men to make the impact as the leaders of the home. There is no way around it, my friend, and you are needed for a refreshing influence. Some men may say they do not go to church frequently, attend church rarely or possibly not at all. There are others that have absolutely no belief in God. I refuse to be irresponsible by dispensing a uniform situation for every man and his household regarding his spiritual life. But I will not defer from my understanding of our need for God's providence within the family. Until that happens, the responsibility is still on men to get a host of things together for their families. I'm no exception. When we make past errors, it may be a formidable mission for years trying to overcome them. However, our thinking needs to be in the right place for our wives and children. Improper focus is a result of human limitations and negligence, but improper influence is a willingness to replicate limitations and negligence onto unsuspecting valuable people.

CHAPTER 16

— *** —

Deal with Problems at the Early Stages

LAUGHING AT INFELICITOUS things will send a nebulous message in the direction of our children. Be careful! There are too many things overlooked that need our immediate attention. Moreover, your character could determine whether you create serious errors in the life of your child. If you emphasize a message of "Do as I say" instead of "Do as I do," then you have been remiss in your deeper communication. The message will be clear to your children that as a parent your words are unequaled to your actions. As a result, there could be a level of respect loss and a perplexing message conveyed to them. It is an important matter to honestly confront. Reflect for a moment. Can your children depend on actions over words spoken from you? I trust we all have work to do. It is true that our lifestyle speaks much louder than empty words. Do you influence by words only or through the application of principles, values and morals? How can we attempt to alleviate setting our children up for failure?

Let me take time to address the latter question. Do you even realize that we can set our children up for failure? If we are not receptive as parents with accepting our natural tendencies to make parenting errors, then this could be a difficult issue and topic. It only means we are not perfect parents. Yes, we absolutely have flaws as parents. I want to be very clear before proceeding with addressing the question. We are witnessing parents and children experiencing disconnection and devalued family partnership more than I can ever remember.

It is not only limited to parents, but there are tremendous breakdowns among many authority figures and their rapport with young people. Guess what? The young people are not always the core reason for the meltdown within relationships. Select your reason for the parent and young person disconnect. In my generation, we basically grew up with the mindset that parents, teachers and authority figures were to be respected. Parents taught us to respect our elders at all times—no questions asked or you were in for some type of correction. As I grew up, those values in the community appeared to fade away, especially going into my early adult years. What happened?

Over the past several years, I have experienced numerous times when the child is confused because of the mixed messages given by parents on a regular basis. So I certainly know we can set our children up for failure when we do not have our standards in order. Your influence will be either productive or unfavorable. Choose and work toward the former. Remember, I'm not talking about being a perfect parent. Impossible!

Let's entertain some specific situations where fathers set sons up for failure and ill-equipped relationships. Brothers, we will absolutely need to impart greater wisdom on our sons pertaining to communication, work ethics, friendships, acumen in finances, respect, love, normal life occurrences and crucial personal matters. I also commend the brothers who are preparing sons to be astute for future family life with their wives and children.

Fathers have a responsibility to put our sons in the best moral, spiritual, psychological, physical and emotional positions. Also, let us not be so judgmental of the errors regarding many fathers, because you may be next in line. In addition, if you are not a father or guardian it will be complex attempting to understand the dynamics of raising a son. So take the time to seek God now for wisdom in fatherhood before marrying your lovely bride.

Premarital counseling was beneficial for me and my wife. I'm blessed to still hold onto some powerful premarital teaching from Dr. Reverend White in Philly. However, marriage and family life carry a substantial deal of on the job training. You can take that to the bank. Do not give up. Marriage was intended for a lifetime. We need more brothers who will endure until the end.

Some additional errors for setting our sons up for failure include teaching lust, materialism, disrespect, immorality, lack of self-control and hypocrisy, to name several deficiencies. This is a brief list to draw our attention to the desire to raise our sons without prioritizing the value of his future. Name your own list, and address it thoroughly. There are various reasons for these errors, but we benefit from being diligent and disciplined in the pursuit of family structure as God intended for us.

I would rather take the time to deal with things at the early stages, so the structure of my family will be in a position to build on a strong foundation. Oftentimes, we are too premature with moving on to the next matter before resolving a possible family catastrophe. In many cases, when we allow things to fester, they usually lead to additional problems. So it will require us to address things on the spot. The ability to invest time in working through a setback brings value and results that we do not always comprehend in the moment. Do you address matters during the early stages or wait until it accumulates into something bigger? I have discovered while working on the problematic areas in my son's life, it also allows me to simultaneously deal with some of my poor habits. The influence of dealing with things during the early stages puts you in position to endure for the latter stages with him.

J.D's Pet Peeves

J.D. frequently shuts the bathroom door when it is not occupied downstairs. He has this thing about keeping the bathroom door closed every time he walks past it. I do not have to tell him to close it behind him, it seems like second nature for him to keep it closed. J.D. can be preoccupied with other activities, but he will instinctively complete his chore of leaving no bathroom door open downstairs. When positive habits develop, I find it just as influencing to follow the lead of children. There are some things that are inexplicable regarding the phenomenal things with our children that we have not necessarily spent time teaching them.

Putting on socks! I remember feeling frustrated on a number of occasions until I was willing to make adjustments in my own thinking. There were times when I was in a hurry to get J.D. dressed and prepared for the day after his shower. However, he had one thing that bothered him about getting dressed. J.D. was never satisfied until his socks were aligned perfectly on his two little feet. I thought that I would never get past this stage with him. Do you ever become impatient with your children regarding values you are trying to instill in them? J.D. was aligning his socks perfectly, because dressing properly was instilled in him. We must be careful not to teach our children to do the right thing and then penalize them for doing it. I see this negligence occur in many homes, and I have certainly been guilty of similar parenting malfeasance.

I'm no psychologist, and I do not have to be one in order to recognize personal parenting errors. There are times when we send mixed messages to our children and blame them for our shortcomings. I implore you to avoid being dishonest, unapproachable and irresponsible toward your children. In addition, challenge, confront and comply with becoming enhanced in your parenting skills. It is not time to self-condemn, feel horrible and soak in self-pity as a defeated parent. Take action! Rectifying the sock situation was fairly simple for me and J.D. I allowed him to put his socks on the proper way while I waited for him. As a result, I averted frustrating him, and he became even more efficient at putting on his socks.

When situations are mundane to parents, we may want to consider the magnitude of importance that it could have for our children. At times, the ability to influence will require you to re-evaluate the seemingly unimportant activities of your child and transform them into a significant development in your rapport with them. It can start with socks aligned perfectly on their little toes or a hat fitted to their style on their little heads. Influence them from head to toe. Just Influence! More importantly, let God first influence you for the most effective results with them.

Brushing his teeth! I'm expecting some good dental reports from the dentist because of J.D.'s brushing and flossing practices. He enjoys sweets like any other child, so my wife and I simply monitor the candy intake with our children. I never get enough of him asking me if he can brush his teeth. He asks to brush immediately after eating a piece of candy. No prompting necessary! Good habits matter! Coincidently, our children never make a big fuss about candy, but they enjoy the opportunity to have it at a moderate level, especially at carnivals or amusement parks. However, it is more to good dental health than not eating candy or chewing gum. Although I'm no dentist, I listen intensely to our family dentist's insight. He makes it clear that all types of sugar can be harmful to our children.

The dentist suggested that too much fruit, juices and other sugary products could be detrimental to our children's teeth. Sugar does not discriminate even with some of the healthier foods. Most parents already know this information, so I'm not telling you anything that surprises you. However, I encourage you to use the information conveyed by professionals and apply it to your daily choices. The results of good habits with grooming and dental hygiene continue to amaze me with J.D. Take notice of the precedent that you establish with your children early in life and the consistency that you teach through an exemplary lifestyle. For some children, influence derives from watching parents give guidance through actions without the need to say many words. Therefore, your ability to see shiny and healthy teeth from your children may just be a matter of personally practicing the things you preach.

I love the influences that have been started at an early stage with J.D. He enjoys competing with his big sister, Azaria because he wants to win at everything. You heard me correctly. J.D. enjoys trying to defeat her at anything that his childish mind can imagine. Can you relate to sibling competition? Use it to your advantage through creative measures. For example, J.D. wants to go first, so his sister will not beat him at various games. He usually attempts to get the best position with games and other fun activities. So my wife and I figured we would creatively implement some special responsibilities with a competitive outlook. We sometimes have the same line of thinking when it comes to the children. I know other couples experience those moments.

Anyway, we tell J.D. to jump in the shower before his sister beats him at taking a shower. His competitive juices begin to flow. It does not need to be reiterated. If he thinks that he will have the edge on his big sister then he is all in. It works, and if we are creative enough, then we will find ways to assist our children with being productive through innovative thinking, responsible behaviors and positive attitudes. Attempt to flourish as a team and do not fall into the delusion that it will never work out for your children. It may require parents to transform your attitude, character, speech and other practices for better results. In my assessment, influence has a greater probability of reaching its target when it is aiming with an eye that looks back at self.

In my experience, it takes courage, trust and confidence in God to expose personal weaknesses, flaws and neglectful areas in your character. When making your life vulnerable to other people, trust God's wisdom for those He desires you to confide in. Not everyone has the wisdom to assist you in pertinent life matters. In fact, there are times when informing the wrong person will make situations worse. Be wise! In addition, the teaching of self-examination is a primary tool utilized with Azaria and J.D. Why? If you constantly practice being accountable, then you gain the advantage of not perpetually making others a personal scapegoat. Why not start them with beneficial qualities at a young age? I'm grateful for Azaria understanding reasonably well certain leadership characteristics and she does not usually become bothered by most of J.D.'s antics, competitive ways, pet peeves and flaws. But there are other times when J.D. exhibits great leadership and teaches all of us something new. Influence is not a matter of age but a matter of hope coming alive.

Teaching Financial Prudence

Azaria has several jars for economic awareness, financial foresight, and becoming a shrewd steward. The correlation of teaching Azaria to save money and my ability to build a savings as an adolescent derives from Chester. It was so natural to implement a system of building a financial plan for Azaria because it was instilled in me. Chester gave me the insight, and I was willing to apply his wisdom to gain useful knowledge. The jar system for Azaria will soon be passed on to J.D. I trust that influence should have a pragmatic value and carry with it the potential to become a stable foundation for the benefit of others. Why keep a good thing to yourself? When influencing a young person, attempt to motivate them beyond the remnants of your ability. Give them something that is sound, responsible, vivacious and full of substance.

The jar system can be labeled according to the attributes your child needs to become influenced according your standards. If you understand that saving money is paramount for your child's life then begin with a savings jar. You can also develop jars for church giving, school spending, helping the needy, lunch, toys, movies (that will help parents) and all relevant economic matters for your children. I trust you get the point. There is no specific jar formula. If you need 10 jars with different labels to implement economic prosperity for your children, then make it work. Whatever you manufacture with the array of jars for your children, utilize God's wisdom and teach it to them. It will not only become teachable moments, but it will also deliver guidance for pivotal matters that could influence for a lifetime. Can you visualize the greater purpose in spending quality time with your children teaching them stewardship? I also encourage you to become creative and allow your teaching methods to be child friendly. We do not want them to see it as another insipid "project" coming from parents. I'm still learning the various innovative ways to become effective in these areas. You may find yourself as a parent learning some new financial tools from your own child.

Listen Artfully

True influence never cultivates selfishness and smothering the progress of others. Do not engender jealousy, pride, envy and distrust. The willingness to influence will require strong listening skills, compassion, wisdom, discipline and personal modifications as warranted. Those characteristics are vitally important especially when we are teaching others. Have you ever definitively knew the answer to something and refused to listen any further to what a person attempts to express to you? In other words, you shut down as the influencer. I have made this error too many times. Although, I really do highly enjoy listening to the wisdom of others, there are certainly times, especially with my children, that I have been remiss in using superb listening skills. When you listen with an ear of discernment then you might discover factual insight that you originally dismissed. Listening at that level demands a high measure of respect toward subordinates, children and mentees. It is beneficial for influencers to pay attention and not devalue other people based on the perceived insignificant status of others. Learn to enjoy the art of listening and effectively engaging your children. Talk less! Listen more!

Avoid Bailout

We should be careful of the bailout syndrome as parents. Influence through bailout is an ingredient for unhealthy, undernourished and uncomplimentary parenting. Do we really understand the current and future harm done to our children through the constant avoidance of embracing the truth with them? "Bailout" is a term I use to identify those situations when we are attempting to provide our children with security, but we actually subject them to a failing position. Bailout can come as a result of being your child's best friend instead of best parent. It may derive from something you missed out on as a parent and think you must compromise essential values with them. I think that is a very popular bailout. You do not want to say no because your child's peers are doing it. Bailout can be a matter of the fear of being perceived as a tough parent. Therefore, you do not follow through with your gut feeling toward your child. I trust the Holy Ghost gives us those gut feelings, but it is up to us to respond accordingly. Can you relate to the bailout responses?

Have I bailed out during my parenting years? Yes, I have absolutely crossed the bailout line enough times. No excuses! Many fathers can relate to this next statement and situation. "It is so much harder to come down hard on our daughters compared to our sons." I believe we are just wired to be more sympathetic toward girls. In addition, there are many men who were taught as little boys to never hurt girls. Chester taught me through his exemplary ways with my mother to never harm females. I know it had an enormous impact on my view toward girls as an adolescent. Thanks, Dad. Conversely, many young boys learned harmful treatment toward females directly at home and as men are ill-prepared to handle conflict with the opposite sex. Do not give up if you were dealt a tough hand in your early childhood years. The Lord does not view you as incorrigible. You can be transformed and not just reformed. Now, you have a deeper reason to transform your ways as a man. Why? Your son will need to become prepared for the proper treatment of females directly connected to your influence. *And Jesus said, [You say to Me], If You can do anything? [Why,] all things can be (are possible) to him who believes! (Mark 9:23).*

There are times when emotions must be contained in order to exhibit the best parental practices with Azaria. However, I feel confident that I'm doing a strong job in my fatherly duties with her. In addition, I recognize various spiritual, natural and practical goals accomplished because of our ongoing teamwork. Azaria works hard along with Daddy to improve certain behaviors in her life. Although there is no pressure to do all things perfectly, I really benefit from the teamwork with my children through prayer, communication and trust. In my estimation, teamwork is pivotal because we will not easily be successful without our children participating fully with our objectives for their lives.

Yet, here is the problem. My struggle is looking in my daughter's eyes while correcting her. It typically causes me to become a little softer with my discipline. Brothers, avoid the eyes. I call it the leniency bone that all fathers have in their bodies for their daughters. We were born with it, and it is adjacent to the kidneys. Ask the doctor to show you that bone in your next examination. Just kidding! But leniency should not convert into irresponsibility. On a serious note, I had to evaluate the weakness that I was depositing into my daughter through not implementing suitable ramifications for her life. Children easily pick up on this parenting deficiency and use it against you. The willingness to bail children out can be a long-lasting problem that needs to be resolved before becoming progressively worse.

The parents who are in denial or totally miss the bigger picture are in a worse position regarding setting their children up for failure. Why? They do not take heed to the damage being done right under their leadership. Our children face additional struggles when we submit to misdeeds, dishonesty and insidious ways through our parenting lifestyle. The problems created are not exclusive to our parenting deficiencies, but it further diminishes other important qualities for our children. There is a thin line between giving our children a second chance and setting them up for failure. I trust that the wisdom of God along with honesty and observing our children will tell us how we are measuring up. Take time to discern God's plan so that you can apply it to your parenting actions.

Assess Leadership in Your Home as a Family Man

What do you see when you observe leadership in the home? Are you satisfied, dissatisfied or precarious about your leadership position in your home? Study, dissect and administer the leadership qualities that are relevant. I trust that it is a valuable component for men to evaluate our leadership in the home. Why? We need vision, perspective, planning and execution of leadership plans with our family. It is so intriguing that we spend substantial time expanding other areas of our lives while neglecting some of the most valuable growth in our homes. I'm speaking for myself as well, and I'm not content with simply expressing these thoughts. I'm working on various flaws, and I'm certainly not ashamed to admit it. Brothers, God will continue to help us transcend our leadership improvidence, inadequacies and improbabilities.

I have not always taken the time to understand the ways to develop as a man of leadership in my home. There are times when we gain insight in our early years, but some prudent ways will manifest later in life. No big deal. Just use it! The ability to develop as a family man demands a measure of honesty, aspiration to transform and spiritual agreement with the family, as well as other men of integrity holding us accountable, to name some of the beneficial gains. That is part of the list that enables me to grow in my family leadership. By the way, do not become deterred, disheartened or dismayed when you have failures as a leader within your family. My concern would be the abandonment of our desire to influence our families perpetually as spiritual leaders. What is your personal leadership list? If you would rather not create a list, then I trust it will still be worthwhile to have a plan of accountability for estimating the leadership position in your household.

I want to address a question regarding our leadership as men. Are we afraid to identify the positive qualities within us? I really trust that many men have not offered or put on display the internal, genuine person. Many of us are enveloped with kindness, compassion, forgiveness…and the list goes on with other valuable qualities. But it is interesting to observe that in some circumstances we would rather not reveal these. There are times when positive men would rather be portrayed as something other than good people. Of course, there are various reasons for putting on such a façade. I know there are situations when we put up our guard, because we are unsure if other people can be trusted. Moreover, it is critical to confront any fear that you are dealing with regarding other men. Influence will never have its greatest impact when one is filled with the mentality of leaving his brother in a state of emptiness. We all have more to give as godly men, including myself, so let us not allow false thoughts to stop us from influence among our brothers.

When we lead properly among our wives and children, then they will get a better picture of our authentic motivation and love for them. Giving them a glimpse of Jesus will allow them to feel the security, safety and trustworthy experience that they desire. The best opportunity to influence with my wife is accomplished through displaying the love of Jesus. I do not know any better way for men to lead with influence among our wives. Lord, I'm grateful for the marriage resolution, and I choose to follow your guidance. *Teach me, O Lord, the way of thy statutes; and I shall keep it unto the end (Psalms 119:33)*

Living Past "Maybe"

The word "maybe" could be a dangerous word to live by on a daily basis. Allow yourself to get the factual information instead of becoming inundated with the numerous possibilities hanging over your head. I refer to this as playing self-psychological roulette. "Maybe it is the correct way or maybe not." When playing this dangerous game, you lose perspective of your intended mission and easily fall off course. In dealing with the "maybe" crisis, too much time is expended on trying to figure out an enigma that has been self-created. You begin to harbor thoughts and ideas that carry no validity or purpose. When you are constantly provoked by the "maybe" of life, then I encourage you to address it quickly. You are not alone, and every person faces some type of insecurity. But do not use that as a pathway or foundation for dealing with every situation. In addition, be careful of entertaining those people who are ill-informed and those who breed confusion. More urgently, do not become one who replicates harmful behavior. Therefore, transform your "maybe" into "I will" move forward to avert maligning others or relegating myself to an uncharacteristic behavior. The influence of "maybe" unceasingly leaves the glass half empty and never reaches its quenching level. *But foolish and unlearned questions avoid, knowing that they do gender strifes (2 Timothy 2:23).*

Group, Social and Miscellaneous Gatherings

Do you agree with people just to be agreeable? There are many times when I have been involved with meetings, gatherings and social situations that opportunities fail to come alive. Why? Many of us have neglected to speak up because of the willingness to go with the flow of everyone else. Can you relate to being uninfluenced because of the crowd? Conversely, I'm not talking about being an agitator seeking attention in front of the group. Use wisdom! I'm referring to those that have done their research diligently and still not utilize their valuable influence. There are times when remaining silent is an important quality, but influence among the crowd may require you to come out of timidity.

As an influential individual, I truly believe it is important to be receptive to correction. Why? We develop in our credibility, self-control and rapport with those influenced by us. Let me ask this question. Do you know people who are in a position of authority, leadership and a high standing rank that despise being corrected with the truth? I truly believe we interfere with further growth and influence when we have outgrown our ability to remain humble, reasonable and rational. Many of us have witnessed people demonstrate great arrogance only to face the reality of their errors at some point. It can be tempting to laugh, desire, and even pray for bad things to happen to others if we are not careful. However, the influence of correction is not for us to use against others. In addition, I admire people from all backgrounds who have made the sacrifice to prosper intellectually within their fields of expertise. I certainly trust that we are able to make necessary strides in relationships when we approach them with diligence, humility and wisdom. Positive interactions from others may not always be reciprocated, but do not reduce your mindset to childish thoughts. *A Soft answer turneth away wrath: but grievous words stir up anger (Proverbs 15:1).*

At other times, you will find people who resent you despite the influence of kindness drenching from your pores. Remember, you are not controlled by their response. (It helps me when I use that particular self-advice.) Self-advice is some of the best individual guidance, but it needs to be constantly applied to our lives. Many people have the resolution to their personal troubles, but they neglect to follow through on applying action regularly. You are not a loser. However, you have lost perspective on the purpose of godly insight, advice and influence being placed in your heart. It was meant to be used for your advancement, hope and liberty. Do not neglect your ability to self-influence because of your inclination to drag along life-draining attachments.

Positive influence will not always receive good responses from others, but it was meant to distribute the good the Lord inserted into your system. It will be tested, challenged and frequently dismissed by those intended to benefit from it. Influence was created to move forward without accolades, celebrations and awards. Some of the greatest abilities to make influential progress are contingent on unselfish motives. Influence is similar to marriage vows. You will need to remain married to it during the good and bad times. In sickness and in health! Furthermore, influence was not meant to be abandoned because one person does not comprehend the future value and payment (not necessarily financial) associated with your investment.

Unfortunately, there are top-notch influencers who reject hearing substantive correction from those they view as beneath them. You can hear the frustration, resentment and intolerance in their response toward their "subordinates." Allow me to express an example of an arrogant response: "I resent that you would even mention that to me." Influential individuals who become unnecessarily defensive because of their personal shortcomings disqualifies them from reaching their target group.

As long as people are not behaving in a vindictive, disrespectful or degrading manner, then we should welcome fresh and competent ideas. Sometimes those fresh concepts will be contrary to yours as a leader. It is not personal. I find it hard to respect the influential position of someone always trying to exert their power improperly. When leaders are non-receptive to appropriate criticism then it may speak about some hidden insecurities on their behalf. By the way, do you continue to work on your personal impediments? As a result, you will become an improved listener, mentor, father, friend and human being.

CHAPTER 17

Favorite Influences and Personal Insight

Favorite Person to Listen to In Life

MY GRANDMOTHER (BIOLOGICAL father's mom, Inez is 92 years old, and she continues to press on in life. I do not get to see her in person frequently, but many times I have enjoyed sitting at her side just listening to her talk. The influence of a grandmother sharing stories, which are intertwined with historical events, wisdom, tradition, compassion and scripture deliver personal refreshing outlooks for a grandson. My grandmother expressed to me that she would rather listen to me talk during our conversations. However, I not only love listening to her, but I relish being in her presence. Her favorite saying is "Keep on keeping on." One of her normal influential scripture references *If we live in the Spirit, let us also walk in the Spirit (Galatians 5:25)*.

Conversing for Longevity Through Phone Calls

I'm really not a person who desires talking on the phone for long durations. But I do make an exception to talk for extended times to a few people. I have a great friend, Sister Rosie in Philly who graduated from college with me many years ago. Every time we talk on the phone my wife and I understand it is going to be a long conversation. Sister Rosie is extremely respectful and courteous toward my limited available time because of my family life. I still recall the many laughs regarding our similar challenge with a college course and supporting each other with class notes. She has been a mother figure for me ever since our college days in Philly and she poured wisdom into my life during critical years. I will always be thankful for Sis. Rosie. She is a friend that genuinely desires to see all people prosper. Some of her greatest qualities continue to be her determination, compassion, honesty, loyalty and love for the Lord. The next time we talk on the phone it will be time to shut everything down and catch up for an extended period. The influence of talking with a friend that loves the Lord is worth every second of the two hour conversation.

Favorite Influential Song

The **Artist**-Victory in Praise Music/Arts Seminar Choir
Song: **Stand!**

The song encourages, validates and empowers me to take a stand, even during the seemingly impossible circumstances of life. In addition, taking a stand will cause personal tears, obstacles, broken relationships and pain. But God will ultimately see us through. Just Believe!

Words do not describe the power this song brings to my life. In addition, I must acknowledge that I'm grateful for many of my friends being willing to support God's move and transformation in my life. Also, I'm indebted to so many friends who travelled with me or came to encourage me during my preaching days in Philly.

Influence to Last for Years

Have you ever been imbued by someone years after the initial situation? I can still remember my late non-biological father, Chester, affecting me with certain words. He would tell me, "You never know what you may have to do in life, so try to learn everything possible." He was so correct. Some of his additional influences which continue to impact me years later include the following. It was instilled in me to be a hard worker, and it continues to have meaning for me today. I enjoyed Chester's calm demeanor, family leadership, cooking skills, productive methods, sacrifice and an obvious love for humanity.

As fathers, if we are willing to commit ourselves to investing in essential values on a consistent basis, I trust that we will observe our sons utilize influences early in life. In addition, the impact will be substantive and be of the long-term value for our sons. Consistency really matters! I experience a positive longevity influence with J.D. because of teaching, re-teaching, patience, love, trustworthiness, commitment, adjustments and on-the-job learning. I'm not claiming mastery, but I absolutely acknowledge profound productivity between father and son. There are many fathers who have experienced the benefit of being respectful leaders in their family lives. Therefore, be encouraged to influence not only your son but the next generation of boys. Influence that can significantly impact our young men years later should be considered priceless at this present time.

I highly appreciate young people that live in wisdom, purpose and integrity. When encountering young people with such attributes, it is a wonderful sight to behold. If you pay attention closely, you will observe these young leaders in the community, church, school and miscellaneous places. Their language, smile, disposition, thinking, response and purpose make them noticeable among the rest of the group. For the record, I was not one of the consistent stand-out positive youngsters. I chose my own pathway too many times and then encountered disastrous results on some occasions. It was a waste of valuable time for me, but I'm extremely grateful for restoration. With God it is never too late to become an influencing individual with purpose. I yielded to my opportunity for Christ-like living starting in my mid-twenties. I really want to be clear about whether your life will transform in a positive manner when you become older. Growing older does not guarantee that you will utilize wisdom. We have all witnessed adults with the immaturity and mindsets of a teenager. Conversely, I observed some young people with the wisdom of an adult. I could possibly have been stuck in the former category without conceding to God's purpose and plan for my life.

I also value the positive influence that young people have on their peers, because it really sets a strong precedence toward a renewed high standard. I call those particular young people one thing: Courageous! It takes heart to take a stand in the midst of popular choice and overcoming the crowd. The ability to have foresight while applying it regularly in your life will reduce improvident vision and unnecessary trials. There are times when young people are not equipped with that foresight, but productive influence applied years later speaks volumes about the influencer.

We also understand that some influence that affects us years later is wrapped in harmful apparel. What detrimental influences from your past hold you captive today? It may not be a major inhibition, but it continues to lock you in a progressive languish within your mindset, heart, spirit and emotional condition. I encourage you to sincerely consider the influences that affect you years later. Influences that are unduly linked to your heart can deceptively drain the life out of you. There are times when individuals are troubled constantly, because they are incapable of shaking off the things that torment them.

In a recent conversation with my wife, I mentioned my gratitude for being delivered from so many issues. As a young man, I enjoyed gambling, because it was an early influence, extremely accessible and in many ways addictive. There were many struggles growing up that I was not aware of having a potential negative impact on my life. No excuses! It was always a choice to surrender to selfishness, ungodliness and problematic forms of life. I also did not care many times, because it felt so much better doing things the wrong way as a lost young man. That mindset and stronghold over my life costs me valuable time, energy, regretful setbacks and harm to other people. Even still, no self-condemnation! Losing valuable time as young men will never be recovered and in some cases could be a lifelong challenge. So never undermine the nonsense being spoken into the lives of young men. It's not just about ideas poured into their lives for the moment, but the impact of the influence that occurs in the future. The willingness to invest unrelenting uplifting ethics into the father and son influence sets the stage for a lasting foundation. Keep building on it, brothers! We can do it.

I have witnessed people relegate their health to a poor condition due to former deplorable circumstances that continue to attach to their lives like leeches. All influence is not good influence. Reflect on the things that still stunt you moral, emotional, spiritual and life growth. There are also various things that I should have done a better job at in life. However, I try not to imprison myself for past errors. It benefits us to utilize the wisdom of others.

Perhaps, we will use it years later. Influence has a lasting impact. Lord, provide us with the wisdom to revel in influence that impacts our eternal purpose.

What is My Story?

We all have a story and it is important to not be ashamed of your shortcomings, flaws and imperfections. So I will give a moderate version of my story. Throughout my life, it was usually important to become successful at something. As a young man, I especially aspired to do well with business, sports, educational pursuits, friendships and eventually a dependence on the Lord. Ultimately, I trust the core of my story to be infused with God's ultimate purpose for my life and a willingness to surrender to it. Many people may have similar encounters. Although, I do experience some regrets over former actions as a young man, they never weigh too heavy on my life. Why? I really trust that things happen for a purpose. We need to become awakened to the reason we go through our story. Could I become the man that I turned out to be without the errors, mistakes, bad relationships, pain, unwise choices and influences? No! I had to travel this journey and ultimately come to terms with God's greater influence for my life.

If you are precarious, embarrassed or broken in your character, then people and the enemy of your soul will use your insecurity against you. *Be sober, be vigilant; because your adversary the devil, as a roaring lion, walketh about, seeking whom he may devour (1 Peter 5:8)*. Therefore, I'm stating that my story does not define me, but it continues to assist me in my life determination. I really trust that it is crucially important to find out the things that motivate you internally and do something with it. Although I will acknowledge having many negative tendencies as a young man, I still had an affinity for the so-called underdogs of society growing up. I imagine that many people can relate to rooting for the underdog. People do it all the time in sports. Similarly, it had meaning for me to care for people struggling with overcoming obstacles and needing someone to cheer them to victory.

The issues could range from mental health illness, drug problems, academic struggles, moral deprivation, physical illness or individuals needing a listening ear. I enjoyed supporting the seemingly less valuable members of society. More importantly, when I was able to grow spiritually and supersede many selfish behaviors, then I was able to broaden the population of people to serve. It did not matter whether they were young, middle-aged, older, healthy, wealthy, educated or ordinary human beings. The mission was to uplift, demonstrate compassion and encourage them to move forward in life. My wife has told me on a few occasions that I have empathy for people. She expressed to me the way I carry the burdens of others in my heart. Our personal story can draw us to influence without fully considering parameters, boundaries and limitations.

If you had the knowledge to change your life at anything that was deemed necessary to improve, would you do it? Do not be so hurried to give your answer. Of course, most of us would desire to rectify the problematic places in our lives. However, that was not the question. Would you be willing to make the change through your actions? In some cases, we are not willing to change. There are times when I can identify those habitual setbacks and recognize my limitations. That is when I use one of my favorite sayings. "There are just some things that I will never be able to accomplish without conceding to God's will." It is a great spiritual, practical and life influence for me when I apply those words to the difficult areas of my life. Application of the Word has been the difference maker with moving beyond the crucibles in my life. Recognizing shortcomings does not guarantee that a person will do something about it. Being comfortable with problematic areas in life can lead into a lifestyle of complacency. Influence can be deceptive, especially when you are self-motivated to resist "getting out of your own path of destruction."

At other times, people do not want to modify poor life influences because of various reasons. One reason is people do not want to change their lifestyle. Another reason is that it feels comfortable taking shortcuts. We develop habits that are not easy to overcome. Consider your own non-impactful habits, so you can relate to the substance of the original question. We all have them, and some poor habits are worse than others. We are not always willing to make necessary life changes, because it feels like too much of a burden. You are probably putting too much focus on self. I love to re-focus during these situations and make necessary spiritual, mental and practical adjustments. Can you relate to feeling weighed down about constantly attempting to do the right thing without good results? Better yet, do you feel trapped in a life of unceasingly doing the wrong thing? Do something about it. I'm bringing all of these life challenges to the forefront for a few important reasons. First, there are some things that are more powerful than your mental and emotional strength can handle. Second, you will benefit from God's influence over your life. No filters required for those two resolutions!

Better Than "Normal"

I want to mention a recent observation regarding eating habits and the challenge of doing a better job for my physical health. For many years, I have been reasonably disciplined in my eating habits, especially in my early years as a boxer. There was a period in my life that I stopped eating red meat altogether for approximately 10 years. When I started eating red meat again, it did not seem like a big deal. By the way, let us remain willing to address all poor habits that extend beyond our eating struggles.

However, I recognized on a deeper level several months ago that eating certain foods really makes me feel better. Of course, this is not a revelation for most of us. When I stopped eating red meats in the past, I continued to endure a multitude of headaches on a normal basis, because I consumed too much sodium. Although I was not eating red meat, my health did not always feel the best. The insight from my younger cousin, Dawn, in Philly to constantly watch sodium intake gave me a renewed physical and mental life (no more headaches). However, it still comes down to one thing moving forward while being influenced with things you definitely realize are life changers for you. Take action. What are you going to do regarding knowledge, insight, and information that you recognize are vitally important for your wellbeing? There is certainly a level of ambivalence in many of our choices. For example, I usually eat in a healthy manner, but I still consume a few unhealthy foods. I occasionally eat red meat (mainly hamburgers), but I know that I can feel so much better without consuming them. Is it a no-brainer not to eat them? You decide. I know it should be a matter of doing the right thing for healthier living on a personal level. The right influence can sometimes *feel* like un-influence. Unfortunately, people wait until something radical happens before taking control. Case in point: We know that we have not been feeling well because of poor eating habits. Yet we wait until we have an appointment with the doctor to tell us the obvious. He or she tells you the same thing you have been saying to yourself for years. Yep, you guessed it. "You need to change your eating habits."

Sometimes influence comes down to adhering to the guidelines of those more qualified than you. I greatly appreciate those who have researched and become experts in their respective fields of work. However, we do not have to wait to hear the experts affirm the palpable health defects we are facing. The doctor does not constantly need to enlighten us about the risk of smoking, lack of sleep, unsafe sexual practices or the results of not taking care of your health. You already know the truth. Therefore, we benefit from using common sense along with a measure of influence from God's word. In addition, I say, "We are not always willing to be influenced about doing the right thing, even when we undoubtedly know it propels us to better living. There are too many times when we would rather take the capricious, dangerous and perplexing route of life." I feel a level of gratitude when God empowers me to make the proper personal decisions that will benefit me as well as the lives of others. I was discussing with my wife the importance of doing things for my family that I potentially would not otherwise feel galvanized to achieve on my own. I have experienced being in a position many times doing things better than ordinary because I was able to think, respond and consider the welfare of my family. Influence involves your commitment to being compelled to do better for the sake of your integrity toward others. I call that "finding a way to improve."

Know Your Personality

I think about myself as a reserved person. Although I have a job that requires me to talk frequently, I also extremely enjoy listening to other people. There are times when I can be overly quiet, and I think it conflicts with my affable nature. Unfortunately, people can misinterpret quiet ways as being anti-social. So I try to make adjustments when necessary, but I do not think it is wise to talk too much without listening effectively. Conversely, I become more talkative when engaging in faith-oriented conversations. Talking about the Lord encourages me greatly.

I have always been very competitive whenever I desire to be the best at something. For some reason, I thought that I could defeat my non-biological father, Chester, in checkers when I was an adolescent. He was just too good for me, but I would desire competing with him until he broke my confidence. My competitive nature has transitioned to the game of chess. Approximately 20 years ago, I persistently pursued learning the game of chess through competing and reading chess books. There was a time when I quit playing chess, because I became addicted to the game. It consumed too much of my time while I was simultaneously pursuing other endeavors, such as graduate school. But I have not lost my competitive nature. I especially loathe losing at chess.

In sports, like many other competitive young men, I did not handle losing well. Mostly, I desired to win against others either individually or as a team member. I have always been this way as long as I can remember. Being competitive certainly carries with it certain advantages, but it could potentially be harmful without containing a measure of proper perspective. There is a childhood friend of mine in Philly, Terrence who could always beat me at any sport, and I continued to compete against him for years to no avail. In hindsight, he probably made me a better competitor and played a part in my attitude to never give up. Competition between he and I was very intense as youngsters. I recall when we would transform a game of Nerf basketball into an outright boxing/street fight/basketball match. The headaches endured after those battles still makes me cringe today. Although I would usually be on the losing end of our competitive games, I would leave his home only to compete with him at something else another day. The influence of friends has purpose, even during seemingly superfluous, competitive childhood games.

In competing with others, I would usually keep playing until I found a way to win or come back the next day to compete again. When challenging bigger guys—and usually that was the case for me—I actually felt confident about winning. Being short and thin was a combination that I became accustomed to accepting in sports. It may appear that you are somehow disadvantaged, but your internal influence will put you in a position to surpass your adversaries. The same mentality motivates me with my work with young men. But it is now elevated, because I continue to grow in my understanding of God's purpose for my life. In addition, my big sister,, Sabrina always had my back while growing up, and she was concerned about my wellbeing in high school because of my size. No problem! I typically had an advantage many times, because I was usually quicker than most guys due to my smaller stature. So I teach my mentees to use their God-given abilities and understand the qualities (not just physical) that the Lord gave them.

* * *

CHAPTER 18

Stay Aware of Non-meaningful Words, Expressions and Other Non-influences

FAKE IT UNTIL You Make It. This is self-explanatory on so many levels. Too many times we are encroached upon with images that are immaterial, superficial and counterfeit. Why should we perpetuate being a fraud? Personally, it is so liberating to experience satisfaction with the person in the mirror. Faking anything brings about a certain mentality that attaches itself to the person. Also, be extremely judicious in sharing personal information and photos with the whole world. It may be the root of your faking. If this is you, I know transformation awaits your life. You are not a loser, and Jesus offers life and life more abundantly.

I Made It. Most of us have used this term in some fashion when identifying success in business, life, material acquisition and other miscellaneous achievements. Be Careful! I have come to realize that "making it" is not exclusively symbolic of the outer things attained in life. I Made It because of the things I have been willing to surrender in Christ. Liberating Influence!

Kill Them with Kindness. I prefer saying, "Bring them to life with kindness." There are truly times when people are not genuine in their kindness. Have you ever encountered individuals who are really being sarcastic with their kindness? Most times you can see right through their shallow manipulation. They really would like to hurt, provoke, destroy and kill with their factitious kindness. So "Bring them to life with kindness" means it is a heartfelt desire to see others prosper and rise above their condition.

You Get Wiser with Age. I totally disagree with this empty saying. Unfortunately, I have seen people become substantially worse with age, because they are trapped in their desire to lead a life of selfishness, non-productivity and discounting of the truth.

The Devil Made Me Do It. People too frequently use this saying as a way to avert responsibility with life. It enables them to constantly run from the truth and put the blame on the enemy of their soul for everything. Although, I understand the enemy comes with a purpose of destroying us, you should not pile all your malfeasance on the enemy. It is such a liberating experience to be honest with yourself!

I Have Done My Best. I believe those words are misused by many of us. Have you ever mentioned that you have done your best? When do you know you have done your best? How do you measure it? In my estimation, we under-value our abilities because we have become satisfied with tricking ourselves into thinking we have done our best. This does not mean that you have not put serious effort into becoming successful in a particular area of life. But it does mean you have not necessarily met the criteria for doing your best. Why is this even important? In my case, I recognized that I was not correctly evaluating my ability to accomplish at a higher level. I would say that I'm doing my best, but in most cases it was far less than my best. Too much self-dependency also prevented me from excelling to a greater plateau. The ability to optimize your endeavors is possible when you reduce your time in self-indulgence and move toward the greater plan approved by the Lord.

We can use words that appear to maximize our achievements, but in actuality we are not meeting the highest standards. There are also times when we have selected words such as the following: "There is nothing else I can do," or "I have extended myself as much as I can." While there could be some verac-ity in those statements, in too many circumstances we simply refuse to go any farther. Conversely, it could be true that you have given your best. But there is a greater power, reserve and overflow within you. Tap into it! Allow yourself to distinguish between God's best within you and adhering to your personal limitations. I have been guilty of this countless times. But influencing at our highest point requires an honest perspective, self-evaluation and walking in the truth according to what God empowers us to accomplish in life.

So we are being self-deceptive without understanding its impact on our mental, physical, spiritual and emotional tenacity. I'm simply saying we usually have increasingly more to offer, but we become complacent because we have frequently depended on stopping at a certain point by stating "I have done my best." Have you really done your best? The ability to influence with the proper attitude and heart will take you far beyond mediocrity. In addition, this type of influence would prefer to optimize through God's wisdom, courage and fortitude. I want us to envision doing our best from an updated lens. You will become mindful of whether you have earnestly exhausted your best efforts or put too much effort into exhausting yourself (self-will).

When doing your best, it is always inextricably linked to God's best. How do I know? I questioned a young man recently about doing his best subsequent to him experiencing some conflict at school. He assured me that he wanted to "do his best" with repairing the relationship with a young lady. So I asked him if he were willing to give this young lady a card or letter to express an apology for disrespecting her. He made it clear that he was not ready for such an approach. In my assessment, it is better to come in contact with your limitations and acknowledge them immediately rather than manufacture false statements about unrealistic goals. That was progress for the young man. There are times when we verbalize that we have done our best and we have not even come close to attaining such a level. It is imperative to identify whether we are really doing our best at any endeavor. Why? Because, we can ascertain that we have no possibility of achieving the highest level of success without consulting with the truth of God's word. We limit our capabilities through loosely using words, which we have habitually used out of convenience, distortion or being under the illusion that we are pursuing our top-notch abilities.

In my personal life, I'm grateful for many of the unforeseen struggles with leading a blended family. I would not want to take back all the personal flaws, trials, heartaches, frustrations, misunderstandings and many additional adjectives concerning my development within a blended family life. No pressure!

In addition, there were many errors made on my behalf with my older children, Imani and Decor. It really helped me to learn ways to become better prepared for raising my younger children. I distinguish errors from mistakes.

In my perspective, "mistake" means that an action or communication was genuinely an accident without any premeditated thought. Conversely, I view "errors" as the part of my humanity that often gets led by ego, pride, overt masculinity or working from my limited power. But I have become more equipped, committed and determined throughout this journey of confronting errors. Just to be clear, I never feel compelled to attempt living an error-free life. Not possible! When we have errors, it is a matter of working on the personal defective ways of our lives. Furthermore, God has filled me with an attribute to "never give up" from my days as a youth. However, you will not see me mention that I have mastered family life, because I trust that being a leader within my family is an ongoing work. I'm captivated by the many new spiritual, natural and practical matters that enhance my family life at unexpected times. I also give *major props* to my children, especially my older kids, for understanding that an imperfect father is still learning ways to influence through God's best within me.

I must acknowledge that learning from my errors along with the Divine power of God assists me to move beyond the difficult circumstances of life. Determine your outlook on mistakes and errors, but never allow it to victimize your life. If we are not careful, we fall into the trap of incarcerating our minds based on former errors. So I earnestly appreciate our older children for teaching me valuable parenting lessons during our early years of family life. I encourage all brothers who desire to lead and influence your family to seek the Lord's forgiveness and trust Him to bring life into those situations that you are incapable of handling on your own.

Do Not Become Un-influenced

The ability to promote un-influence is an interesting dynamic regarding our daily communication. Remain aware of your willingness to easily succumb to negative dialog, thinking or actions because of the un-influence of others.

There are many times that people will dictate the conversational flow and impose their derogatory view of life. Do not judge them. I trust that some of those situations derive from an unintentional and habitual discontent with their personal outlook. If you do not clearly understand an individual's need, trouble or shortcoming, then restrain yourself from hindering them at a deeper level. If possible, help them out.

How do you handle or mishandle those un-influencing situations? We all come across these moments. Furthermore, I feel like a magnet that attracts people who feel like releasing their personal information. There are times when I feel qualified to respond and other times it exceeds my scope of experience and knowledge. Be honest with yourself. Know your gift. I'm grateful for two important attributes for addressing those needing to release their pain. Patience and a listening ear have been beneficial in many of the impromptu dialogs. Stay alert! It is easy to get dragged into un-empowering, un-influencing and un-intelligent agendas. Even when you do not intend on saying negative words, the impulse can still arise in you quickly. In other words, do not put people in a worse position subsequent to their leaving your presence. Seriously! Do not allow your influence to transition to un-influence because you refuse to take a stand on honoring God in your conversation.

If you become a victim of those conversations, then do not beat yourself up. We benefit from remaining aware of the degrading ability to become un-influential. How frequently do you engage in conversing with others before you begin talking in a negative manner? There are times when people will influence you with the negative energy experienced in their hearts. Think about it. Have you ever felt influenced by nonsense that is contrary to your character? We do not ask to be put in these situations, but it is frequently necessary to handle them effectively. We should place a premium value on guarding our hearts. In addition, some of my personal tools are fleeing from self-damage, self-harm and self-temptation. For me, it is not always a physical fleeing. I seek ways to utilize transcendent thinking, transcendent action and God's wisdom above all.

How do we assure ourselves that we do not become a statistic of promoting further un-influential dialog? I want you to carefully consider your answer, technique and resolve for engaging un-productive communication.

Furthermore, we either know people who are always thinking from a negative angle or encounter them in our daily routines. If you reflect deep enough, you may find that you are a carrier of un-influencing communication on a regular basis. No problem. Take action! I love when we can acknowledge our weaknesses and determine to make a change. The effective measures of influence become more profound subsequent to spending quality time in self-examination, self-reflection and an in-depth depletion of selfishness.

Let me insert an important point about my personal perspective on engaging others in typical communication. I have learned that influencing others is not a matter of putting pressure on me to make people view life through my lens. For me, it has become simple. It all starts and ends with depositing important matters on the shoulders of Christ. I'm not in the business of trying to make people think similar to me. There can only be one authentic Leroy Martin. Likewise, there can only be one genuine you. Furthermore, I'm reasonably successful with maintaining unflappable focus during challenges of communication.

Allow me to refer to my days in Seminary School. My faith became so shattered because of many challenging religious encounters that I was absolutely not prepared to handle. I still recall vividly the days I cried to myself on my drive from the Howard University Campus in Washington D.C. back to Virginia. However, in time, my faith became increasingly restored, and I learned to think, communicate and develop more love for God in my heart. Many of us have experienced some long nights because of the travails of life. When a person is affected by un-influence it can be more powerful than influence. Conversely, if you are able to withstand an un-influential whirlwind, then you are more equipped to influence without being enveloped by life's intense moments. So I value the obstacles, hardships and challenges that persist while attempting to influence through my communication. Do you frequently succumb to un-influencing practices? You are the one who can adequately address that question.

In my work with many families, it only takes one family member to make things toxic for the remainder of the family. It is one of the greatest reasons that I trust in the leadership of a godly man within the home. As men, it is not sufficient to just show up at church and never apply the word of God at home. Additionally, it is extremely valuable when God's word lives through us in all environments. The family can discern your sincerity as a leader, and they will respond to it accordingly. I did not say that there are any perfect fathers, so erase that from your expectations. But we are encountering some unprecedented times, both good and not so good, within our homes. Fathers are the game changers, and I will not deviate from that mindset. Furthermore, we should never forget the beautiful brides that are the helpmeets.

We do not have to look far to understand the challenges with attempting to maintain a peaceful home. In fact, you do not need a family counselor to understand that all families endure some measure of un-influence within the home. Therefore, we all benefit from identifying, modifying and executing on enhancing family leadership. One of the greatest communicative family experiences in my home occurred approximately seven years ago. What was this great family experience? Family meetings! I still appreciate the influence, insight and value of family sit downs and gatherings. You do not have to label them family meetings or give them any formal name. The meetings were extremely instrumental in learning, growing and addressing essential matters for my family. I highly encourage all families to benefit from the influence of individual voices within the family. You may hear some unflattering things, but we are meant to be courageous and confront the challenges within our family. The problems will not dissipate magically, but you are assured to gain new insight with the right family approach. I'm looking ahead to the privilege of participating in family dialog with our two youngest children.

In my personal assessment, the greatest influences that occur for our children initiate at home. I do understand the impact of secondary influences, and that is the reason I emphasize the significance of felicitous influence at home. There are definitely times when I feel extremely concerned with the many troubled experiences confronting our children. I have not mentioned the social media aspect attacking our children. If parents are ill-equipped, then it will add to the detriment of our children. In fact, I would say most of us as parents are facing some uncharted waters regarding this current generation. Do I think there is an abundant level of pressure our children are experiencing? Absolutely!

There are people who try to influence from a place of intimidation, fear and embarrassment. Insecurity from an influencer as well as the one being influenced can heighten this problem. Although we all have insecurities, it does not mean we are inept. When people are uncertain about their potential in life then it could possibly result in allowing others to define you. Have you experienced relationships that you have outgrown? Not because you are better, but you are able to detect the non-influence in the situation. In some circumstances, people have harbored this type of mentality from their youthful years. Do not begin pointing fingers at everyone else you label as the problem. I will acknowledge that some of my shortcomings as a young man were not addressed appropriately, and the problems forwarded into my adulthood. Sound familiar? If you do not identify the non-influences that have inhibited your life progress, it could take more time than necessary to work through them. In addition, you leave the door open for influences from the wrong people. They try to rule from a place of insolence, control or superiority. Their persuasive power influences you easily, because you are willing to settle for anything. Do not surrender or substitute your influential ways because someone leaves you feeling incompetent. Know that God has called you to become something great, and you are not characterized by the degradation of others.

Restricted Feeling

Let us be cognizant of not reducing our lives to a meaningless portion because of limited resources. I'm sure most of us are familiar with the saying. "keeping up with the Jones's." In addition, when you irresponsibly compare your wealth to your neighbor's wealth, then you will self-influence in a defective manner. In other words, be content, satiated and pleased with your resources. The Lord absolutely wants us to be good stewards. So we should not be shortsighted with our ability to become productive, stable and responsible regarding our resources. We have also seen this comparison of making our children better than somebody else's children due to education, abilities, groups and other apparent status-oriented living. If you missed it the emphasis is on the word "better." I seriously think it is an error to create a mentality of superiority versus inferiority, especially among our children. If you have been guilty of relegating others to an irrelevant status, then reevaluate your thinking right away. You will discover that negative outlooks impede you from being unrestricted in your value for humanity. Restricted influence means you availability toward others will remain beneath its intended purpose, productivity and potential.

Reading Between the Lines

I equate reading between the lines as potentially being irresponsible in your approach to getting to the truth. There are certainly times when we feel that we understand a person's intention by reading between the lines. Assumptions can put us in a bad position. It reminds me of the popular saying, "I'm not a mind reader." However, we often play the mind reader as an adjunct career in various circumstances. I do not get involved with social media because of my personal choice. But many misunderstandings, assumptions and destructive scenarios arise out of reading between the lines. Why should we avoid reading between the lines? I would rather have the facts and leave the guessing out of the equation. There are people that thrive on making others feel insecure through purposely sending out negative or ambivalent messages. Do not get caught in that trap. If you assume you know something, I encourage you to go to the next step by getting factual information. It makes a difference. Reading between the lines may cause you to misrepresent your own character. The influence of reading between the lines will oftentimes leave you falling one line short of the truth. Seek the truth because it is always in front of you. *For flesh and blood [men] have not revealed this to you, but My Father Who is in heaven (Matthew 16:17).*

Be Aware of Opening the Door

Anything can come in when we leave the door open (literally and figuratively). If we reflect on the many influences in our world, it requires us to look beyond the surface. The willingness to compromise from politicians, parents, ministers, doctors, lawyers and every leadership position imaginable appears to be on the rise. Big time! I do understand that some things require a spiritual discernment to understand the total context of the future circumstances and its impact on our lives. However, there are many circumstances that are not nebulous, and influential people are going with the flow despite the ramifications. I know it is not always easy to take a stand. But if you open the door to nonsense, it brings with it the stench of depravity and all of its partners. I want to really impart this to your spirit so that you will keep a watchful mind on the influence and power of opening the door to anything. If you accept anything and compromise on most things, it will create a lifestyle of instability. *A double minded man is unstable in all his ways (James 1:8).*

Do you ever feel like you open the door for subtle problems? I implore you to be honest with your answer. Your problem with opening the door to trouble and being controlled by selfish agendas could be a matter of not utilizing your "way of escape." We really do set ourselves up for failure at times. We walk right into the same stuff purposely with no plan of allowing the Holy Ghost to lead us. We frequently put too much self-trust in our decisions. The influence of "opening the door" to anything could "close the door" to your most important thing. *I am the Door; anyone who enters in through Me will be saved (will live). He will come in and he will go out [freely], and will find pasture (John 10:9).*

I acknowledge opening the door to obvious obstacles for my life too many times. Have you made the same error in your life? The devil did not make me do it. The Lord gives us a choice, and I want to make that clear. Repentance in our lives releases us from the bondage. What are you going to do about opening the door? Be aware of the self-inhibition, self-deceit and ongoing self-hostage position ruling your life. Close the door to inadequate, un-holy and lackluster influences consuming your life.

Watch the small things, because they can become the bigger problem. The people we influence are also entangled by what we allow to come into our lives. Allowing anything to creep in usually puts us in a position to cross boundaries. In doing so, it becomes a battle recovering from crossing certain lines. Give some thought to the ongoing power of influence due to allowing anything to enter your heart. Going too far will bring with it equivalent repercussions. Some of us notice it with our families, politicians, church, school and other societal dynamics. You may not be able to prevent events from happening, but do not let those same harmful influences control your mind. The influence of allowing anything to enter our lives will extend beyond us. The compromising of leaders puts those depending on us for influence in a vulnerable position. What and who are you being led by in life?

CHAPTER 19

***

Personal Influential Sayings, Thoughts, Spiritual Assets and Observations

IN MANY CASES, people are imbued, influenced and affected by something that delivers meaning to their lives.

We can retain the great things in life by giving them away. Something greater always comes as a result of your unselfishness.

The bigger picture must sometimes yield to the smaller picture. Similarly, the smaller picture at times will take precedence over the bigger picture.

Become addicted to good habits, such as love, peace, hope, truth and other scrupulous matters, and you could be hooked for life.

Our children need us to give them judicious ramifications to assist them with making prudent life choices.

The only one that can stop me is me. Jesus is in me. Therefore, I am unstoppable.

Do not always work on perfections but also confront imperfections. Similarly, work on imperfections to help you enhance your perfections.

Attempt to leave an individual with a sense of hope despite the wrong done to you by that same person.

Life is like the game of chess; think several essential steps in advance to make paramount life moves. Avoid myopic vision.

Work on one or two major life impediments at a time. Do not become overwhelmed. Be earnest and diligent when facing your deficiencies and goals. Time resolves many issues.

Face all fears. Run to your fears and deal with them while leaning on God's Vows. Peace will ensue (*Psalms 56:1-13*).

Do not allow yourself to be incarcerated mentally or emotionally due to personal poor habits or the flaws of others.

Until you have put some earnest sweat, tears, aspirations, persistence and determination into accomplishing something, do not think you have mastered the task. Subsequent to success, maintain humility.

Examine yourself to discover what God is saying to you regarding correction, transformation, and moving forward in this life's journey.

Do not allow your good health to be destroyed by worries regarding your attachment to material, monetary or tangible items.

Be accountable, and prevent yourself from placing the blame on others. Watch the dangers of pride. It is extremely toxic and venomous.

A community is partially based on its current resources, values and people. Help a community change for the best by investing in those areas.

It is a choice to get angry. Conversely, it is a choice to love.

Think!

Take Action!

Pursue dreams and goals. Utilize an incentive to live vivaciously daily. What is your motivation for today?

Every day, do something that brings you joy, makes an impact or delivers some significant value to your life or the lives of others. It does not matter the size of the deed.

What does it take to be successful? How do you measure it to ensure ongoing success?

Be watchful of the specific things that you are enamored with in life. For example, lust of the flesh, lust of the eyes and the pride of life. (1 John 2:16)

Do not become lured by the misery of others.

Ruminate on His word, love, peace, grace and hope.

Just because someone treats you horribly, it does not entitle you to reciprocate similar behavior.

Study God's word and more urgently use and apply it to your life.

We can't permanently change the deficiencies of others. God does the real transformation. Learn to accept the weaknesses of others and do not allow it to negatively impact you or your attitude toward them. Pray Earnestly!

Be careful of what you expect from others and your desire to control them in subtle ways. It is extremely dangerous. There is a fine line between control and guidance.

Love all people in spite of their actions or circumstances. *(1 Corinthians 13:1-13)*

Always be prepared to make adjustments.

No pressure!

Really Be Original

We become so firmly fixated on reiterating the thoughts of others without utilizing personal creativity. It does require discipline and other attributes to break those copy-cat habits. There are various times when we do benefit from gleaning from others. However, I find myself thinking outside the forest. I know you thought I was going to say thinking "outside the box" Right! I enjoy being creative enough to come up with my own sayings. Why? There is no more space to become someone else because it is already reserved for that person.

Do Not Wait

We respond too late. Proactive living puts us in a viable position. We frequently fight harder when something attaches itself to us. Do Not Wait! Be alert with your spiritual, emotional, psychological and physical health. We all benefit from living the right way and not just reacting to detrimental circumstances as they occur.

You Have All You Need

Why do you prefer to chase the dreams of others instead of evolving in the advantages within your life? We should be careful of coveting the things of other people. Relish in what God has entrusted to you.

There Are So Many People Sitting on a Gold Mine

The gold mine to which I refer is the wealth of liberating information that people refuse to make applicable for their life. Have you ever listened to a person give you some extraordinary advice and the same person never utilizes the information for their personal progress? I call that the greatest self-influence that never happened. Why does that occur? For many reasons and it depends on the personal story of the individual. One of the bigger issues is an individual's reluctance to completely surrender to God's way. They remain stuck while others are becoming un-stuck. We could spend substantial time addressing the previous challenge, but I encourage us to consider seeking the Lord's wisdom in an diligent manner. Influencing others with sound advice should have a component that involves usability from the owner of the advice.

Optimize Influence

I love being honest and realistic regarding the people we are entrusted to guide. I have discovered faults in my personal work through placing limitations on the outcome of a situation. Although I work on not putting too much pressure on myself, it helps enormously when I identify and sincerely work on moving beyond my flaws. In addition, be aware of allowing personal annoyance to become your reason for devaluing the lives of others entrusted to you. I refer to it as the influence that got away. Optimize influence. Strive in a deeper fashion, because your limited view will create additional insecurities for the one you were meant to help. Ironic!

Move Beyond Trepidation

Answer this question. Would you help a person with a difficult situation if you were going to possibly embarrass them? How far are you willing to go to encourage an associate? People are not consistently receptive to influencing others even when you know you have precisely the resolution for their life alteration. Too much fear, selfishness and other reservations preclude us from helping others with attaining their freedom. You were meant to influence, but your faith will need to be chased by action. Catch up with your faith before it leaves you stranded without conforming to your God given purpose. *Then He said to His disciples, The harvest is indeed plentiful, but the laborers are few (Matthew 9:37).*

Stay Informed

Be slow to speak. Move forward with the proper instruction and influence. Get the facts, information, knowledge and wisdom God holds for your life.

Be Influenced by the Right Things

Why do I want so many material things? Why does it take "things" for me to become satiated? Have you ever experienced people that are not content with life unless they have something monetary or materialistic? It is a factitious way to live our lives when things unduly control our thoughts, choices and ability to maintain peace.

Identify Influence Correctly

"I would rather have what belongs to you because of misidentified influence." Many words could come to mind regarding this statement. Choose one—envy, selfishness, covetousness or dissatisfaction! You may have a few more adjectives to add to your personal list. Your influence has been shaken because you have chosen personal influence above God's influence. We should be cognizant of selecting our personal gain above the gain in Christ. I'm determined not to move for the sake of looking good among other people. Some would select the opportunity to move ahead in a worldly manner above living a life of rest and peace. Our lack of visionary thinking, improvidence and defective mindset prohibits us from envisioning the deeper message. If this is true for you, you have preselected, predetermined and premeditated on the wrong choice. Do not feel ashamed. I simply want you to be aware of your aptitude to surrender to things that were not intended for your consumption. So if you are constantly overtaken by the status, talents and resources of others, then you are disconnected with the potential prosperity attempting to arise in you. When you flourish at something, it will not always bring forth an outward, visual or glamorous affiliation. In short, you may covet the property and lifestyle of others, because you do not understand the value associated with your original purpose, plan and destination. The gem (figuratively speaking) that God inserted in you continues to be customized for your life. Do not dismiss the beauty of your character, attributes and purpose. There are times when individuals influence others based on utilizing an artificial influence that never initiated from them. It will not deliver the same results. Just be you!

You have all you need to remain successful. Why do you pursue the advantages, accomplishments, dreams, assets and privileges of others? Stop doing that! You are equipped with God's best and do not forget it. The influence placed within you was customized for your life. Use it prudently and judiciously. Trust Him!

Define Tough Love

I must acknowledge that I grapple with this term, but I firmly think it brings substance when applied properly. This particular phrase is clothed in oxymoron attire. What do you refer to as tough-love? Some may say when dealing with various situations regarding our children and you become exhausted with the struggles of your child then the only thing left is tough love. Others may express tough-love in a manner that symbolizes love that does not allow others to take advantage through enabling actions. Some may refer to it as loving your child with restrictions attached. You may have a totally different meaning. No problem! Many people have expressed the usefulness of the "tough love" method. Does it work for you? There are times when parents are at a point when they feel there is no other alternative with their children except to give them tough love. They have attempted everything else to persuade their sons or daughters to do something with their lives but nothing seems to work. In these situations, they will release their enabling attachment with their child and respond with a transformed love.

I do understand the context of the saying. In addition, I think tough love can work with the appropriate applied system. But I just prefer to separate the seemingly conflicting title. I love because I need to love. I'm firm when I need to be firm. Remember, it is not about being right or wrong but using effective methods. I referred to tough love many times in the past to describe the approach to dealing with difficult situations with our children. Whether you agree or disagree with the saying is not up for debate. Are you really giving tough love? Are you just being tough with no sign of displaying love? Certainly, there is a time to be firm in our communication, dealings, response and actions. There are situations that require me to be assertive in my dealings with J.D. Say what you mean and mean what you say. It appears more beneficial to separate love from being tough. However, I will not argue with anyone effectively using the tough love method because it has a place in relationships. If influencing with tough love appears counterproductive, then try independently putting them to work in your imbuing skillset. Whether you use tough love or separate the two methods, make sure to influence with a measure of intentional objectives.

J.D.'s Favorite Commercials

J.D. enjoys the former football player from Chicago Bears, Icky Woods. The commercial plays out something like this. "Whoa. Number 44, that's me. Hey, lady. I'm going to get some cold cuts today." Woods goes into his football dance. It is a catchy commercial. I also find myself paying attention when the commercial comes on television. It really makes me laugh when J.D. and Azaria imitate the commercial together.

He also enjoys the many commercials with "Flo" from Progressive Insurance.

J.D.'s Favorite Songs

Song-"When Jesus says yes, nobody can say no."
Artist-Michelle Williams Featuring Beyonce and Kelly Rowland
He really enjoys expressing his love for Jesus and that song motivates him.

Song-"Gotta Have You"
Artist-Jonathan McReynolds
J.D. exhibits sincerity, joy and inspiration to others when he sings this song. His eyes light up and he gets caught up in his own world as he expresses those words of praise.

When J.D. was in the shower recently, he started singing some words from an old rap song–(Rappers-Fat Boys) The rappers mention the words- "Too hot to handle and too cold to hold." I remember just a few words from the song and decided to say them to J.D. as we were getting his shower water going. He never heard the rap song prior to me saying those few lyrics. But I would just say those words to him, and J.D. began using it as his shower theme song. Humorous Influence!

Pull Out the Power Within

J.D. puts his hands on his head and heart. I mention to him that God is always near. I appreciate professional athletes pointing to the sky to acknowledge God. But I enjoy teaching J.D. the Holy Ghost resides within you and the Spirit of God is never distant from your life.

Speak the Language of Influence

There are encouragement words which are identifiable for those that need to be uplifted. I enjoy finding ways to express gospel words to others on the spot. Our ability to utilize the language of influence transcends the face to face dialogue. There are many times when I e-mail other people with language, such as "have a peaceful day." "May your day be filled with joy!" "Keep on trusting!" Why does it matter? It matters to me, because I do not want to abandon or relegate my ability to influence in a loving manner to Sunday morning only. Of course, we will need to use wisdom in our interactions and language. If you attempt to proselytize others, it may come with ramifications. I'm not implying for us to ever walk in fear, so continue to travel with God's wisdom.

He never makes an error. Somebody needs to be influenced with the jargon of comfort, peace, truth, hope and love. Language matters!

Pray

For a long time a meaningful prayer life escaped me. Better yet, I avoided a willingness to pray consistently with my heart settled on prayer. Moreover, there is still so much to gain in my current prayer life, so I continue enjoying my prayer growth and development. The ability to influence according to God's calling in my life requires communication with the Master on a frequent and consistent basis. When quality prayer takes place in our lives we can move with a certainty that God is in control and His sovereignty never fails. I'm also grateful for connecting in prayer with Brother Michael for the last few years. Those who are earnest about praying can compel you to experience prayer life in an unparalleled manner.

Rely on the Incomparable

There is nobody that influenced better than Jesus. He influenced all types of people. Jesus demonstrated the ability to affect children, the sick, the lost, destitute women, the deprived, the broken, liars, murderers, thieves and especially me. Although He influenced others, I'm first grateful for the salvation that comes from accepting Him as Lord and Savior. What can be a better influence than eternal assurance with the Father and Son? *That if thou confess with thy mouth the Lord Jesus, and shalt believe in thine heart that God hath raised him from the dead, thou shalt be saved. For with the heart man believeth unto righteousness; and with the mouth confession is made unto salvation (Romans 10:9, 10).*

Acronym

Focused
Attentive

Trustworthy
Honorable
Effective
Reasonable

Special
Obedient
Noble

————— ✳ ✳ ✳ —————

Epilogue

FATHER AND SON influence is not limited to a father's experience with his son but should be a conglomeration of influences that serve to solidify an influence in your lifetime and for future generations. The ability to write *Father and Son Influence* is due to the influence of the Father, Son and Holy Ghost power.

The weight of your influence is contingent on the weight of your sincerity with your son. Your son can identify when you are producing superfluous and empty words of influence. In addition, our goals for our son's life should never replace God's truth for his life. Do you value the relevance of God's sovereignty in your son's life? My ability to move from ordinary influence to extraordinary influence is always a matter of my earnest relationship with the Lord. As a result, the weight of your influence should unremittingly remain connected to God's purpose during the *Father and Son Influence.*

Influence in all areas throughout the father and son voyage. We are not limited to one particular sphere of knowledge. Your acumen in sports, business, construction or art should not preclude you from seeking God's wisdom with influencing your son in a different arena. Some parents have the tendency to impose their will on their children. Our ability to pray and trust God for salutary results with our children is essential. Allow your unconditional love for your child to lead you beyond the ordinary influence in all environments.

The quality of your influence matters substantially. Do you ever consider the quality of your influence? There are certainly times when we all neglect doing our best. We should be vigilant to avert giving poor quality in an irresponsible manner due to laziness and other unhealthy habits. In my estimation, the actions of fathers usually outweigh his words. Know your shortcomings, deficiencies and flaws in life. I have discovered that learning from my limitations puts me in a better position during the father and son journey. Why? I use it as an opportunity to solicit grace, peace and necessary help from the Lord. Every man will encounter some limitations within the family life with your wife and children. However, you and I become qualified family men of influence when we are willing to surrender to the Father of Influence. Be compelled by Jesus then go and compel someone else in His name.

In my present *Father and Son Influence* journey two scriptures have especially elevated my actions.

And be not conformed to this world: but be ye transformed by the renewing of your mind, that ye may prove what is that good, and acceptable, and perfect, will of God (Romans 12:2).

Let your conversation be without covetousness; and be content with such things as ye have: for he hath said, I will never leave thee, nor forsake thee (Hebrews 13:5).

Thrive in the Word that brings relevance, healing, clarity and transformation for the *Father and Son* journey. And Remember This! *All scripture is given by inspiration of God, and is profitable for doctrine, for reproof, for correction, for instruction in righteousness (2 Timothy 3:16).*

If the Lord is not your SOURCE then you will constantly undervalue, under-nourish and under-appreciate all other influential sources. LJM

I would love to hear from you about *Father and Son Influence*. Please email us your comments about this book at the address below.

Elitementoring@hotmail.com

26271925R00136

Made in the USA
San Bernardino, CA
24 November 2015